ONE-MINUTE
Stewardship

ONE-MINUTE
Stewardship

Creative Ways
to Talk about Money
in Church

Charles Cloughen Jr.

CHURCH
PUBLISHING
INCORPORATED

Church Publishing
19 East 34th Street
New York, NY 10016
www.churchpublishing.org

Cover design by Jennifer Kopec, 2Pug Design
Typeset by PerfecType, Nashville, TN

Library of Congress Cataloging-in-Publication Data

Names: Cloughen, Charles, author.
Title: One-minute stewardship : creative ways to talk about money in church /
    Charles Cloughen Jr.
Description: New York : Church Publishing, 2018. | Includes bibliographical
    references and indexes.
Identifiers: LCCN 2018000863 (print) | LCCN 2018015088 (ebook) | ISBN
    9781640650091 (ebook) | ISBN 9781640650084 (pbk.)
Subjects: LCSH: Christian giving.
Classification: LCC BV772 (ebook) | LCC BV772 .C568 2018 (print) | DDC
    248/.6--dc23
LC record available at https://lccn.loc.gov/2018000863

ISBN-13: 978-1-64065-008-4 (pbk.)
ISBN-13: 978-1-64065-009-1 (ebook)

Printed in Canada

Contents

Acknowledgments

Thank you, thank you, thank you to all who assisted in making this book possible. It would not have been published without the hard work and help of:

- The Rev. Elizabeth Masterson, who supported me in writing this book. She was my primary editor and helped with formatting the meditations, rewriting my "Theology of Stewardship," and patiently encouraging me along my journey. Without her this book would not have been possible.
- Mr. Milton Brasher-Cunningham, my editor at Church Publishing who has worked with me to make this book a reality. Without his help this book would not have been published.
- Bishop Eugene Sutton, who has written the foreword, and who invited me to become the Director of Planned Giving, Stewardship, and Development in 2009. His support has been unwavering in my work.
- My beloved wife, Judy, who encouraged and supported me in my ministry for some thirty years, and who entered eternal life on January 10, 2014.
- My children, Chad, Tamara, Teresa, and Wendy, who have emotionally supported me in my writing of this book.
- Mr. James Murphy and Mr. Ken Quigley, who have supported my work in planned giving in the Episcopal Diocese of Maryland.
- Ms. Pamela Wesley, director of advancement at Berkeley Divinity School at Yale, who mentored me for some eight years in the importance of personal relationships in stewardship.

- All those who wrote the meditations on giving, stewardship, church year, special occasions, and planned giving that are a centerpiece of this book.

I want to thank the following persons who have inspired, nurtured, and taught me the essence of stewardship as well as the value of personal relationships these past forty-eight years—"Thank you, thank you, thank you:"

- The Rev. James Annand
- Adam Barner
- Mary Blair
- The Very Rev. Rob Boulter
- James Byers
- Oscar Carr
- Thomas Carson
- Charles and Anna Cloughen
- The Rev. Roy Cole
- The Rev. Canon David Crockett
- Hugh Davies
- Tom Gossen
- Kathy Grayson
- Phoebe Griswold
- Jason Hoffman
- Glenn Holliman
- The Rev. Halsey Dewolf Howe
- Elizabeth Huntress
- The Rt. Rev. Robert Ihloff
- The Rev. Frederick Jellison
- The Rev. Laurel Johnston
- The Rt. Rev. Charles Longest
- Anne Lynn
- The Rev. Michael Mayor
- William McClintock
- Frederick Osborn
- The Rev. Terry Parsons

- The Rev. Kenneth Phelps
- The. Rt. Rev. John Rabb
- The Rev. Ronald Reed
- The Rev. George Regas
- Robert (BO) Rice
- Frank Robinson
- The Rev. Austin Schildwachter
- Dowell Schwartz
- Sharon Tillman
- Charles Wilson

My thanks to the vestries and parishioners where I served my ministry and learned through experience the practice of stewardship.

- St. Martin's Church, Providence, Rhode Island
- St. Matthew's Church, Jamestown, Rhode Island
- St. John's Church, Waterbury, Connecticut
- St. Andrew's Church, Pasadena, Maryland
- St. Thomas' Church, Towson, Maryland
- And the Episcopal Diocese of Maryland

Contributing Authors

The Rev. Stacy Alan
Chaplain, Brent House, the
Episcopal Center at the
University of Chicago

The Rev. Melvin Amerson
The Methodist Foundation,
Austin, TX

Pastor Hilarion Arenas
Tarija, Bolivia, with Five Talents
USA

Mr. Brian Joseph Backe
Senior Director for U.S.
Programs and Resource for
Catholic Relief Services

The Rev. Jane R. Bearden, STM,
Hon.rt.
The Presbytery of Baltimore,
MD

The Rev. Dr. William L.
Bearden, Hon.rt.
The Presbytery of Baltimore,
MD

Ms. Amanda Beyer
Senior Program Officer,
Episcopal Migration
Ministries

Dr. Mary Blair
Chair, Stewardship Team,
Cathedral of the Incarnation,
Baltimore, MD

The Rt. Rev. Joe Goodwin
Burnett
Tenth Bishop of Nebraska,
2003–2011

Mr. Jerry Campbell
Capital Campaign Consultant,
Episcopal Church Foundation

The Very Rev. Stephen Carlsen
Dean and Rector, Christ Church
Cathedral, Indianapolis, IN

The Rev. Suzanne M. Culhane
Canon for Stewardship, Diocese
of Long Island

The Rev. Mary Davisson
Executive Director/Port
Chaplain, Baltimore

International Seafarers'
Center

Ms. W. Lee Dickson
Executive Director, Godly Play
   Foundation, Inc.

The Rt. Rev. C. Andrew Doyle
Ninth Bishop of Texas

Mr. Rick Felton
The Episcopal Network for
   Stewardship

The Rev. Canon Scott Gunn
Executive Director, Forward
   Movement, Cincinnati, OH

The Rev. Canon Jan Hamill
Director, Episcopal Service
   Corps, Maryland

The Rev. Dr. Thomas John
   Hastings
Executive Director, Overseas
   Ministries Study Center, New
   Haven, CT

Ms. Constance Hegarty
Retired Organist and Choir
   Director, Windsor Locks, CT

The Rt. Rev. Robert W. Ihloff
Bishop of Maryland, Retired

Ms. Heather Joseph
Senior Program Manager,
   Foundation Programs,

Episcopal Migration
Ministries

The Rt. Rev. Chilton R.
   Knudsen
Assistant Bishop of Maryland

The Rev. Canon Charles LaFond
Canon Steward, St. John's
   Cathedral, Denver, CO

The Rev. Dr. James B. Lemler
Rector, Christ Church,
   Greenwich, CT

The Rev. Kristen Looney
Director of Partnerships,
   Religious Freedom Center
   of the Newseum Institute,
   Washington, DC

Ms. Anne K. Lynn
President, American Friends
   of the Episcopal Diocese of
   Jerusalem

The Rev. Elizabeth Rust
   Masterson
Rector (retired), St. Nicholas'
   Church, Newark, DE

The Rev. Jeff McKnight
Board Member, Five Talents,
   USA

Mr. James W. N. Murphy, CFRE
Managing Program Director, Financial Resources, Episcopal Church Foundation

Mr. Jim Oakes
CEO, Five Talents USA

The Rev. Dr. Daniel L. Ogden
Retired Pastor, Reformed Church in America

The Rev. Stephen Parker
Author, *Bridges: Embracing Faith and Science*, retired Chaplain, Salisbury School, Salisbury, CT

Ms. Julia Pearson
Canon for Evangelism, Cathedral of the Incarnation, Baltimore, MD

Mr. Will Putz
Director of Development, Five Talents USA

Mr. Kenneth H. Quigley
Senior Program Director, Endowment Management Solutions, Episcopal Church Foundation

The Rt. Rev. John L. Rabb
Bishop Suffragan (retired), Episcopal Diocese of Maryland

Mr. Robert W. Radtke
President, Episcopal Relief and Development, New York, NY

The Rev. David A. Rash
Stewardship Matters, Virginia

Mr. Robert B. Rice
Principal and Managing Director, CCS Fundraising

The Rt. Rev. Gregory H. Rickel
Bishop, Diocese of Olympia

Ms. Kate Riley
Diocesan Youth Missioner, The Episcopal Diocese of Maryland

The Rev. C. K. Robertson, PhD
Canon to the Presiding Bishop for Ministry Beyond the Episcopal Church

The Rev. Margarita Santana
Canon for Latino Ministry, Episcopal Diocese of Maryland

The Rev. Regan M. Schutz
Director of Communications and Development, Godly Play Foundation, Sewanee, TN

Mr. Greg Sharkey
Senior Philanthropy Advisor, The Nature Conservancy

The Rev. Dr. J. Barrie Shepherd
Minister Emeritus of historic
    First Presbyterian Church,
    New York, NY

The Rev. Dr. Laura
    Sheridan-Campbell
Vicar, Holy Cross Church,
    Carlsbad, CA

Ms. Julie Simonton
Officer for Congregational
    Development and
    Stewardship, The Episcopal
    Diocese of Virginia

The Rt. Rev. Eugene Taylor
    Sutton
Bishop, Episcopal Diocese of
    Maryland

Ms. Betty Symington
Executive Director, ERICA—
    Episcopal Refuge and
    Immigrant Center Alliance,
    Baltimore, MD

The Rev. Daniel Webster
Canon for Evangelism and
    Media, Episcopal Diocese of
    Maryland

The Rev. Fred Weimert
Vice President of the Board,
    Central Maryland
    Ecumenical Council

The Rt. Rev. Carl Walter Wright
VII Bishop Suffragan for the
    Armed Forces and Federal
    Ministries

Foreword

I was honored when the Rev. Charles Cloughen asked me to write the foreword to this new book, *One-Minute Stewardship: Creative Ways to Talk about Money in Church.* Eight years ago I asked him to lead the Diocese of Maryland's efforts to raise money to fund our growing mission initiatives. Let me tell you when and how that hiring decision happened; it's a true "God story!"

Charlie had recently retired as a parish priest when he invited me to lunch in June 2009. (Charles had developed a prodigious "invite people to lunch" ministry, and I came to learn from him over the years that feeding people is a very successful tactic for raising money.) He took me to Germano's, his favorite restaurant in Little Italy in downtown Baltimore—which later put up a bronze plaque naming "Father Charles' 'Luncheon Ministry'" as the place in the restaurant where he's always seated. What Charlie didn't know is that a few hours earlier the person on my staff responsible for development had just resigned to take on a new job.

At lunch, Charlie and I got to know each other better, and we talked about what made us passionate about the work we do as church leaders. He told me about the book he published in 1997, *One-Minute Stewardship Sermons*, and how stewardship and evangelism were closely linked—two sides of one coin. He was clearly energized about reaching out to people and funding mission to spread the good news of Jesus Christ. I immediately asked him to be my new Director of Planned Giving, Stewardship, and Development, the position had been open for six hours!

It was one of the wisest decisions I've ever made. Since Charlie began in 2009, we have tripled the total number of our donors through several giving portals and increased substantially the total giving to our various ministries. In 2008, the diocese had 335 donors who gave $95,621 through our annual Bishop's Appeal. In 2015, the last year he was responsible for the Appeal, it had 881 donors giving a total of $214,319.

Charles believes that the basis of stewardship is gratitude, an appreciation for God's abundant grace and generosity. A spirit of thanksgiving underlies it all. He teaches and lives the belief that the key to development are six key words: "Thank you, thank you, thank you!" He is constantly thanking people.

Charles also knows that when it comes to stewardship, "leaders lead." Throughout his time on diocesan staff he reached out to all our new clergy, both those called from other dioceses and those who received new calls to parishes within our diocese. He invited them all individually to have lunch with him at Germano's to welcome them to the Diocese of Maryland. He knows that effective stewardship is rooted in the importance of developing personal relationships. People do not give to programs, but to people.

The response to his personal outreach to the clergy was impressive. In 2008, only 34 clergy gave to the Bishop's Appeal; by the end of 2015 there were 207 clergy donors (almost all of our active clergy and many of the retired ones)—a six-fold increase.

I believe there can be no strong, thriving diocese without having strong, thriving parishes. Effective stewardship must have congregational financial development at its core. An essential part of this development has to be planned giving. When Charlie began his work in 2009, we had a diocesan Legacy Society that consisted of 170 households from 38 parishes. He developed a sermon called "Don't Leave a Mess" that he preached in many of our congregations, both large and small, and conducted workshops in the parishes on "Planning for the End of Life." As of this year, there are now 341 households in 54 congregations that remember their parish (and in some cases the diocese as well) in their wills. Through Charles Cloughen's efforts and the planned giving team he has put together, more and more churches will achieve more financial stability in hard times because more of their members are generous in remembering the church at the time of their death.

This book will give you some of the reasons we have been so successful. These meditations give spiritually based and very practical ways of reminding all Christians of their role in moving forward God's vision for their communities through stewardship. The meditations can be used at the time of the offertory; they can be printed in Sunday morning leaflets, parish newsletters, and weekly parish e-mails. They are also an excellent resource for sermons, containing many good illustrations for solid stewardship teaching.

Instead of writing the book all himself, in typical fashion Charles Cloughen has reached out to church leaders to offer their own wisdom about stewardship. What an expansive model for doing God's work! By incorporating many voices, the book itself models the way that Charlie raises money to further the mission of God: invite everybody to participate in the community of love known as the body of Christ, ask them to do something big for something good, and then share in God's abundance.

To my friend and colleague in ministry Charles Cloughen, please know that these six words flow from my heart to yours: "Thank you, thank you, thank you!"

Blessings always,
The Right Rev. Eugene Taylor Sutton
Bishop, Episcopal Diocese of Maryland

Introduction

One-Minute Stewardship: Creative Ways to Talk about Money in Church finds its basis in three principles:

- The first principle: connect the vision and mission of the parish or congregation with its stewardship. How parishioners use their time, talents and abilities, and their money can make this vision and mission a reality. Thank them for the generous giving of their time, their talents and abilities, and their money.
- The second principle: stewardship preaching and teaching must take place all year long. A parish should not confine it to six weeks in the fall.
- The third principle: generous giving requires creating good relationships and connections.

How Is Your Congregation Connecting with One Another?

Today we live in a world of connection in ways I could not have imagined when I wrote One-Minute Stewardship Sermons some twenty years ago: weekly e-mails to congregants, Facebook, texting, Twitter, and Instagram. These media are connecting people and are changing our world in ways we are just beginning to understand. Today, many congregations have Facebook pages that highlight activities in the congregation and parishioners' involvement in these parish ministries. Parishes can send out e-mail blasts with details on the funeral arrangements for a beloved parishioner or to describe a special event at the church. The incredible feature is that these cost nothing to send out; the only expense is a person's time and talent to compose the e-mail. In some of our smaller congregations, a weekly e-mail from the rector keeps the congregation up-to-date on the ministries that are being done in the name of Jesus. Since many of our parishioners no longer attend every Sunday, the weekly e-mail and Facebook may be the only connections to the congregation. I believe every congregation needs a weekly e-mail that can be used for the teaching and practice of stewardship. My concern is for those who do not have e-mail. I recommend a monthly newsletter to be sent out by both e-mail, as well as through the postal service—for those who don't have a computer. These can have articles about giving and stewardship.

How Are These Challenging Times for Our Church Community to Keep Connected?

Our Presiding Bishop Michael Curry was asked at an event I attended, "What is the most challenging thing facing the Church?"

He answered, "I was on my way to preach at the church of one of my vicars in rural North Carolina. I asked, 'What is your competition: the Baptists, Methodists, or Disciples of Christ?' As we [the bishop and the vicar] rounded the bend, there was a soccer field with several hundred children and parents. And this was in *rural North Carolina* on a Sunday morning."

Sunday morning has radically changed in America. The church has major competition from all kinds of activities. For many, it is children's athletics: traveling soccer and football teams in the fall, and baseball and lacrosse teams in the spring have supplanted Sunday worship. Good parents who value Sunday worship need to say "no" to Sunday morning athletics. But when the championships arrive, parents are hesitant to pull their children off a team they have been with all season. I remember one Pentecost when two of my finest and most dedicated parishioners were off coaching opposing teams on one of the most important days of our liturgical calendar.

Also one finds more people attending various marches for causes like breast cancer, juvenile diabetes, and the environment. They all seem to take place on Sunday mornings. Then one adds weekend traveling for mini vacations and to see family. Sunday is no longer a day just to attend church. This is a challenge to our parishioners' exercise of faithful stewardship.

A church community needs to make every Sunday count and every worship service a celebration of our Christian community. Stewardship needs to be taught most Sundays—in the bulletin, leaflet, or program, at the offertory, occasionally in the sermon, and especially in the weekly e-mail for those who are not in worship.

What Then Should We Do to Teach Stewardship?

Back when I was ordained in 1969, churches would focus on a six-week stewardship program beginning in October and ending with an every member canvas on a Sunday afternoon. The rector would preach one stewardship sermon, and two letters would be sent. Following the reception of the pledges, a general thank-you letter would be written. That would be the only time stewardship received attention for the year until next October.

Today we need year-round stewardship education based on a theology of abundance and gratitude. We need to confront a worldview of scarcity, the fear of never having enough of what we need. We, as the church, can offer a different way of looking at our world. When many new members enter the church today, they have no experience of pledging or faithful giving. They may have never been a member of a church community, or they may have been dropouts from another congregation. They often begin as token givers. Over the years, with good year-round stewardship education, they can become generous givers. Good stewardship education grows givers. We all need to be reminded of God's abundant generosity and the need to share it with others through our church's mission and ministries.

One-Minute Stewardship: Creative Ways to Talk about Money in Church provides a resource for pastors and congregations to conduct stewardship education all year long through meditations by outstanding stewardship leaders. These meditations contain illustrations of good

stewardship and generous giving. They show ways to connect stewardship and giving to the church's ministries, mission, and vision.

One of the challenges all denominations, including the Episcopal
Church, face today is demonstrating the need to connect the mission of
the local congregation to the mission of the diocese or other judicatory
structure. Why should the congregation financially support any ministry or mission outside its own community? Some of these meditations
will connect this work beyond the local community with the congregation's mission and vision. By providing a way to link the resources
of many congregations, ministry and mission can be accomplished far
beyond what the local congregation could do on its own. For example,
part of every dollar given in an Episcopal church goes to fund diocesan
work. Then each diocese sends a percentage of their income to support
the work of the Episcopal Church.

It always will be more challenging to connect the congregation to
a national or international church body, such as the Episcopal Church.
Our presiding bishop, the Most Rev. Michael Curry, challenges us to
see ourselves as the Episcopal version of the Jesus Movement. Some of
the meditations in this book connect the local church to the good work
of the Episcopal Church. For example, more than one thousand youth
gather for the triennial Episcopal Youth Event held in various dioceses,
the Episcopal Migration Ministry serves refugees, and various campus
ministries offer care to college students away from home.

We take much for granted in communication with our church members. We tell them once and expect them to remember and integrate the
stewardship message in their busy, complex lives. These meditations are
organized to be used by a rector or pastor, a stewardship committee, the
person who composes the monthly newsletter, the person responsible for
the Sunday bulletin, and the person responsible for weekly e-mail mes-
sages to the congregation.

How Are These Meditations Organized?

- By stewardship theology: these meditations are organized by the
  title of the meditation, which specifies the topic of the meditation.

- By giving illustrations, stories, and vignettes.
- By special occasions: these are organized by parish and diocesan ministries: altar guild, electronic funds transfer, eucharist ministers, vestry, and diocesan support. These can be customized and used to honor a ministry on a specific Sunday, such as members of the altar guild, adult choristers, people who provide the refreshments for hospitality hour. In addition, special occasions will include certain Sundays in the church year, such as meditations for Epiphany or for Palm Sunday. Episcopal Relief and Development, Episcopal Migration Ministries, Campus Ministry, Episcopal Service Corps are examples of ministries that take place for the entire Episcopal Church, but in which individual parish members may be involved. Participation in supporting ecumenical ministries, such as Godly Play, Five Talents, Overseas Study Ministries Center, Seafarers' Center, could also receive thankful recognition.
- By planned giving: these are organized by the ways parishioners can remember their parish or other religious institution in their will or estate plans.

Any of these meditations can be inserted in a Sunday bulletin, in parish e-mail, in the monthly newsletter, or in clergy comments at the offering or sermon.

In summary, my theology of stewardship and the central point of all the mediations can be found in six key words that permeate my book: Thank you. Thank you. Thank you. My theology of stewardship also includes the mantra, "No gift is too large for God's work."

Terminology

I have written this book from my perspective as a retired pastor and a current member of the bishop's staff in the Episcopal Church. I do hope it will be helpful to all who preach and teach the "Good News of Stewardship." To help make the concepts of the book more easily understood by all readers, terms used in the following pages are defined below.

First, the head clergyperson of a congregation in the Episcopal Church is called a *rector* or *vicar*. In larger congregations other priests on the staff are called an *associate* or *assistant*. *Deacons* are normally assigned by our diocesan bishop to a congregation and are responsible for outreach to the community. In the Episcopal Church, we have ordained deacons and priests. *Priests* most often are those in charge of congregations. In many Episcopal churches, priests are called "Father" or "Mother." In some Episcopal churches, priests are called Mr. or Ms. In some congregations, priests may also be addressed by their first names. The choice of the title is up to the priest and the custom of the parish. For the purposes of this book, quite often I use the Protestant term "pastor." It is gender neutral and denotes well the function of our priesthood within the local church.

The *vestry* is the Episcopal term for a parish's legal governing board within the life of a congregation. The church's members elect this board, often for three-year terms on a rotating basis. This body corresponds to such titles in other denominations as trustees, deacons, parish council, administrative board, or session. The vestry calls, with the bishop's consent, the rector of a parish. A *mission* is a congregation that is not self-sufficient but supported by the diocese, and the head clergyperson is called a *vicar*. Church members are called *parishioners*, since in our nomenclature the church is called a parish. In the past, a parish was defined as a geographic area of the church's local ministry, but now many parishioners drive past other parishes to worship at a church with which they feel more comfortable because of its style of worship or its specific ministries.

All local Episcopal churches belong to a *diocese*, a geographical area normally named after a state or part of a state, such as the Episcopal Diocese of Maryland or the Diocese of Southern Virginia. It may also be named after a prominent city, such as the Diocese of Dallas. Our dioceses are headed by a bishop, called the *diocesan*, and elected at a convention composed of all the clergy and elected lay representatives of each congregation. A *suffragan bishop* assists the diocesan bishop and is elected by a similar convention. Bishops are addressed as the Rt. Rev. (full name). The bishop corresponds to the regional head of your congregation's denomination.

The Episcopal Church has its headquarters at 815 Second Avenue, New York City. The Episcopal Church is a confederation of ninety-nine domestic and fourteen overseas dioceses that meet every three years for a General Convention. It is headed by a *presiding bishop*, also called a *primate*. They are addressed as The Most Reverend (full name).

I do hope you will find this book helpful, whether you are a rector, pastor, minister, associate, assistant, worship leader, vestry member, trustee, stewardship chairman, member of your stewardship committee, the person responsible for your Sunday's bulletin or weekly parish e-mail, or just a faithful member of your church concerned about your own and your church's stewardship. Effective stewardship will enable your congregation's mission to change people's lives and make a difference in the name of Jesus Christ.

Section I

Theology of Stewardship

What Is Stewardship?

When church attenders hear the word "stewardship," some immediately tightly grab their wallet or checkbook. Yet stewardship is much more than money. A steward isn't an owner, but is instead a manager of what the owner has left in the steward's care. In a church setting the three things members, as stewards, must manage are time, talents or abilities, and money, including the stuff money buys. Some members practice stewardship well, some poorly. At times members may become anxious about how they are using their time, abilities, and our money.

In sermons I have preached on stewardship in parishes of the Episcopal Diocese of Maryland, I have asked this rhetorical question, "Is there anyone here who has more money than they know what to do with? If so, please see me or your rector following the service and we'll have some ideas for you." Members of the congregation smile and laugh. And guess what? No one has ever spoken afterward to me or to the rector.

Unlike the variability in the amount of money we have, everyone has the same amount of time. We are all given just twenty-four hours a day. Come midnight, today is gone. There are no time-saving machines. All of us have twenty-four hours, no matter how rich or poor we are. As stewards of our time, we are responsible for how we spend these twenty-four hours. Come midnight, if we did not call our mother or our son, if we have not written that thank-you note, or if we have not told our spouse, our children, or our parents how much we love them, these opportunities are lost for today.

In my stewardship sermons, I often ask the question, "How many of you use computers in your work? Please raise your hands." Normally about half of the hands go up. I then comment, "It is good to be with so many people who have to work only 30–35 hours a week for a full salary." I am met with incredulity. I remind them that when computers were first introduced, we were told that with the efficiency computers provide we would need to work fewer hours to complete our work. Of course, this proved to be false. Instead, many people work forty to fifty hours each week or more. We are more productive with computers, but it just means we accomplish more work during those hours. We don't save any time.

I then ask how many took a computer class in college and some hands go up. How about in high school? Fewer hands are raised. Elementary school? The fewest of all. It is very clear that the majority of us learned computer skills after college using the abilities God has given us. In fact all of us, as we have matured, have learned new skills for the new challenges that were not present when growing up: mobile phones, Twitter, Facebook, and Instagram. This ability to learn new things is a gift from God.

Another statement I pose is, "Raise your hand if you don't want to be happy." Never has a hand gone up. I ask, "If we all want to be happy, why aren't we happy all the time?" I don't believe we can will ourselves to be happy. If we wake up and say to ourselves, "I am going to be happy today," and then we go into the kitchen for breakfast and there is no coffee and no milk for cereal, and then on the way to work, a huge traffic jam stalls us and makes us late for an important meeting, our happiness disappears.

Finally, I ask them, "Are you a thankful person? Do you count your blessings?" I challenge them to take the risk and ask their family and friends, "Do you believe I am a thankful person?" I challenge them to take the risk to hear how they are perceived. I firmly believe that being thankful gives us the key to being happy.

Involving ourselves in a church community will offer us the opportunity to become more thankful, more appreciative, more gracious, and more generous. We may become a person who will more fully appreciate God's blessings in our lives. In a healthy church community, a spirit of compassion dwells and works of mercy will be practiced.

The question for all of us who are active in a congregation is, "How much should I give to support God's work in my congregation, especially to encourage the spirit of compassion and to foster the practice of the works of mercy?"

What Is the Biblical Basis for Stewardship?

When I consulted Walter Brueggemann, the renowned scholar of the Hebrew Scriptures, he suggested these texts: the story of God providing manna to the Israelites in the desert (from Exodus 16) and Psalm 145:10–19.

"I have heard the complaining of the Israelites; say to them, 'At twilight you shall eat meat, and in the morning you shall have your fill of bread; then you shall know that I am the LORD your God.'"

In the evening quails came up and covered the camp; and in the morning there was a layer of dew around the camp. When the layer of dew lifted, there on the surface of the wilderness was a fine flaky substance, as fine as frost on the ground. When the Israelites saw it, they said to one another, "What is it?" For they did not know what it was. Moses said to them, "It is the bread that the LORD has given you to eat. This is what the LORD has commanded: 'Gather as much of it as each of you needs, an omer to a person according to the number of persons, all providing for those in their own tents.'" The Israelites did so, some gathering more, some less. But when they measured it with an omer, those who gathered much had nothing over, and those who gathered little had no shortage; they gathered as much as each of them needed. (Exod. 16:12b–18)

The story tells the Israelites to gather an omer of manna every day and on the sixth day gather twice as much for the seventh day, the Sabbath. God's abundance is demonstrated in that each person had enough to eat. But it could not be stored up, because worms infiltrated it and made it stink. God's provision of manna reminds us of the words of the Lord's Prayer, "Give today us our daily bread." We are not asking for more than we need so we can hoard it. We ask God to meet only our needs today.

> All your works shall give thanks to you, O Lord, and all your faithful shall bless you. They shall speak of the glory of your kingdom, and tell of your power, to make known to all people your mighty deeds, and the glorious splendor of your kingdom. Your kingdom is an everlasting kingdom, and your dominion endures throughout all generations. The Lord is faithful in all his words, and gracious in all his deeds. The Lord upholds all who are falling, and raises up all who are bowed down. The eyes of all look to you, and you give them their food in due season. You open your hand, satisfying the desire of every living thing. The Lord is just in all his ways, and kind in all his doings. The Lord is near to all who call on him, to all who call on him in truth. He fulfills the desire of all who fear him; he also hears their cry, and saves them. (Ps. 145:10–19)

The psalmist empathizes with those who are hungry and addresses these words to God, "The eyes of all look to you, and you give them their food in due season. You open your hand, satisfying the desire of every living thing." God's abundant generosity works by providing food as food is needed. Like the psalmist, we need to thank God for our blessings, for his good works.

These passages about God's abundance from the Hebrew Scriptures foreshadow Jesus's teaching about men and women and their possessions (money). He teaches more frequently about people and their possessions than any other subject including heaven, forgiveness, and healing. People living in Palestine during Jesus's time had to pay high taxes, buy food for their family, care for their children, and pay for a home, just like we do. Then, as now, most families and marriages have issues concerning money.

Jesus speaks not about scarcity but abundance. My favorite Gospel story is the feeding of the five thousand. It is the only miracle found in all four Gospels. This is the version found in John 6:1–13:

> Jesus went to the other side of the Sea of Galilee, also called the Sea of Tiberias. A large crowd kept following him, because they saw the signs that he was doing for the sick. Jesus went up the mountain and sat down there with his disciples. Now the Passover, the festival of the Jews, was near. When he looked up and saw a large crowd coming toward him, Jesus said to Philip, "Where are we to buy bread for these people to eat?" He said this to test him, for he himself knew what he was going to do. Philip answered him, "Six months' wages would not buy enough bread for each of them to get a little." One of his disciples, Andrew, Simon Peter's brother, said to him, "There is a boy here who has five barley loaves and two fish. But what are they among so many people?" Jesus said, "Make the people sit down." Now there was a great deal of grass in the place; so they sat down, about five thousand in all. Then Jesus took the loaves, and when he had given thanks, he distributed them to those who were seated; so also the fish, as much as they wanted. When they were satisfied, he told his disciples, "Gather up the fragments left over," . . . they filled twelve baskets.

Five thousand people are fed, and there are twelve baskets gathered of the leftovers. This is abundance, more than enough! The twelve baskets of leftovers provide the central message: everyone ate as much as they could eat and there is still more. However, I have identified my ministry with the young boy who offers his two fish and five barley loaves to Jesus. God has blessed my gifts and enabled me to have an effective ministry. My gifts of body, mind, and spirit, which at times I have felt were somewhat limited, have been multiplied and enhanced during my over forty-eight years of ordained ministry.

Now I offer a bit of humor related to this parable. When I was asked to speak at a Regional Stewardship Conference in the Diocese of Northern California and El Camino Real, I needed a theme and chose the feeding of the five thousand. I knew I could find five loaves of pita bread locally, but I needed two fish. I visited a Korean market and got two salted fish for my visual aids, packing them in my suitcase for the plane ride. When I arrived in California, I found my suitcase was missing. The airline did find it and delivered it the next day. Despite my careful wrapping of the fish, my clothes stank—God's fragrant abundance!

Another example of God's abundance comes from John 2:1–11:

> On the third day there was a wedding in Cana of Galilee, and the mother of Jesus was there. Jesus and his disciples had also been invited to the wedding. When the wine gave out, the mother of Jesus said to him, "They have no wine." And Jesus said to her, "Woman, what concern is that to you and to me? My hour has not yet come." His mother said to the servants, "Do whatever he tells you." Now standing there were six stone water jars for the Jewish rites of purification, each holding twenty or thirty gallons. Jesus said to them, "Fill the jars with water." And they filled them up to the brim. He said to them, "Now draw some out, and take it to the chief steward." So they took it. When the steward tasted the water that had become wine, and did not know where it came from (though the servants who had drawn the water knew), the steward called the bridegroom and said to him, "Everyone serves the good wine first, and then the inferior wine after the guests have become drunk. But you have kept the good wine until now." Jesus did this, the first of his signs, in Cana of Galilee, and revealed his glory; and his disciples believed in him.

Jesus turns about 120 to 180 gallons of water into wine—an abundance of wine—much more than even those guests could drink. Some ask, "What happened to the leftover wine?" I like to imagine we share it each Sunday at the Eucharist.

In Mark's Gospel we find the parable that Jesus tells to illustrate the "largest gift" in the New Testament. When I ask about this in a sermon, someone usually answers (correctly), "the widow's mite." Here it is from Mark 12:41–44:

> He sat down opposite the treasury, and watched the crowd putting money into the treasury. Many rich people put in large sums. A poor widow came and put in two small copper coins, which are worth a penny. Then he called his disciples and said to them, "Truly I tell you, this poor widow has put in more than all those who are contributing to the treasury. For all of them have contributed out of their abundance; but she out of her poverty has put in everything she had, all she had to live on."

Actually, Jesus was not watching but rather listening to what people gave. I understand that offerings were made by worshippers coming up to a large metal tuba-type receptacle with a pipe leading to a safe where the coins were stored. Each would come forward and throw their coins into the metal receptacle. Large coins would make a loud clanging sound. Small coins would only make a ding. In the parable, the widow comes forward and puts in two cooper coins as her offering. Jesus commends her for her gift, because she gave all that she had to live on. As a percentage of her assets, she gave the largest gift in the Gospels.

In my first parish as rector, I had an eighty-year-old parishioner who was, most likely, the poorest person in the parish. She lived in a small cottage, cut her own firewood, and took in laundry. She charged twenty-five cents for a laundered shirt. She was given some land to garden by a parishioner and kept chickens in a coop in her backyard. She sang in the choir, and as she came up the aisle in procession, she held on to each pew for support. Every Thanksgiving, our congregation took a food basket to her home. She pledged and put her envelope in the plate every Sunday. What I found remarkable was every month she put in an additional envelope for the Presiding Bishop's Fund for World Relief, the precursor of Episcopal Relief and Development. She was the only parishioner who did so. She knew what it was like to live to hunger and truly gave the widow's mite. She gave her offering in the spirit of abundance.

Finally, we turn to what I like to call the second largest monetary gift in the Gospels—Zacchaeus's offer to repay people he cheated—found in Luke 19:1–10.

He [Jesus] entered Jericho and was passing through it. A man was there named Zacchaeus; he was a chief tax collector and was rich. He was trying to see who Jesus was, but on account of the crowd he could not, because he was short in stature. So he ran ahead and climbed a sycamore tree to see him, because he was going to pass that way. When Jesus came to the place, he looked up and said to him, "Zacchaeus, hurry and come down; for I must stay at your house today." So he hurried down and was happy to welcome him. All who saw it began to grumble and said, "He has gone to be the guest of one who is a sinner." Zacchaeus stood there and said to the Lord, "Look, half of my possessions, Lord, I will give to the poor; and if I have defrauded anyone of anything, I will pay back four times as much." Then Jesus said to him, "Today salvation has come to this house, because he too is a son of Abraham. For the Son of Man came to seek out and to save the lost."

By committing himself to pay back fourfold those people that he has cheated and then giving half his fortune to feed the poor, Zacchaeus responds to Jesus's acceptance with unbelievable generosity. Is this where today's billionaires get their inspiration? Zacchaeus's relationship with Jesus changed not only his life forever, but also the people to whom he made recompense.

In Palestine and Israel when you are invited for dinner, you do not clean your plate. You always leave a little food on it. If you clean your plate, your host will pile on more food until you finally leave some. There always needs to be abundance—more than enough. God's grace is like that.

How Has the Offering Changed?

In 1997 the offering plate would be passed by an usher, and parishioners would put in their envelopes with a check or cash inside. People without envelopes simply would put in cash or a check. A faithful parishioner was one who attended every Sunday except for illness or vacations. Now a faithful parishioner is one who attends twice a month. The commonly used measure of parish health—average Sunday attendance—can decline even as your parish grows with new families. I found as rector of St. Thomas', where I served as rector of eighteen years, when one of my faithful older members died, I would need a family of three to replace them for the same yearly attendance. And three new families might not contribute as much financially until they understood the spirit of thanksgiving and generosity needed to keep parish ministry vital.

Another interesting take on the stewardship of the church in non-financial terms comes from the Rt. Rev. Chilton Knudsen, assistant bishop of the Diocese of Maryland. She advocates Average Weekly Impact (AWI) as a measure of a church's vitality. Churches should be measured by how they are impacting the community they serve, rather than by just Sunday attendance. AWI means counting those who attend an AA meeting, those who come to a food pantry, those who attend Boy and Girl Scout meetings, and those who attend a Bible study and choir rehearsal. A small church can have a real impact beyond those who gather for worship on a Sunday morning.

There are many more ways the offering can be made to the ministry of a parish today. Some parishioners have chosen to give through electronic funds transfer (EFT), where a specific amount is taken out of their checking account each week, every two weeks or once a month, depending on the frequency of their paycheck, and deposited directly to the church's checking account. There is no cost to the pledger or the church, which is good news for the treasurer: a constant stream of income, regardless of snow, vacations, or illness.

It is important to have something available when the offering plate or basket is passed. The Cathedral of the Incarnation in Baltimore, Maryland, has several green cards in each pew that say "I give by electronic funds transfer (EFT)" and at the bottom in small print, "Contact the Cathedral Office to participate in EFT giving." These are printed on card stock, recycled, and replaced in the pew racks each week. I believe it is important to have something to put in the plate so guests especially can see the offering given. EFT giving is growing each year; one of the touching moments in worship is seeing the children putting in a green card representing the family offering.

Another way the offering has changed: many Millennials no longer carry cash or use checks. They do most of their financial transactions with their credit or debit card. If a church can't accept credit or debit card donations, Millennials may not make an offering. If you can't accept credit and debit card donations, you can't receive their offering.

The Cathedral of the Incarnation in Baltimore, has printed the following statement in the bulletin: "The people remain seated while an offering is received to support the Cathedral's mission to worship God joyfully, care deeply, and act boldly as followers of Christ. An offering may also be made online at www.incarnationbmore.org."

Some large congregations like St. Phillip's Cathedral in Atlanta have installed "giving kiosks" that accept credit and debit card gifts.

Some conservative treasurers balk at the fact it costs about 5 percent to receive credit card gifts. I point out to people who make this objection about the advantage of receiving more gifts by credit card or fewer gifts the traditional way. A church may receive $5,000 in plate offering and pay no fees, but it might receive $10,000 in from credit card offerings as more people choose to give this way. Even though 5 percent in credit card fees will be subtracted from the offering, in which situation is the church better off?

Here's another way giving has changed. I call it IRA (Individual Retirement Account) or 401k giving. Currently according to the IRS, a person over seventy can make charitable gifts from the mandatory distribution of their IRA, tax free. For many Baby Boomers who are now turning seventy, this is a good way to give. Each parish needs to let their church members know that this is possible and how to make it happen.

Special giving may be highlighted at special events, allowing people to give more generously to honor a person or an organization. At a diocesan event—the ordination of our four deacons—the following was included in the service leaflet at the offering: "The ordinands have designated the offering be given to the Episcopal Refuge and Immigration Center Alliance (ERICA). Please make checks payable to "The Diocese of Maryland" or give online at www.episcopalmaryland.org." I see in the not-so-distant future that a rector or vicar will share at the offering, "We need $5,000 more to send our J2A Class to the Episcopal Youth Event," and then announce at hospitably hour, "Through online giving we have raised the $5,000 needed."

How Do You Present Funding the Budget?

The challenge today is not raising dollars for special projects, but for the ongoing budget concerns, such as the rector's salary, the maintenance of the air conditioning, and the diocesan apportionment. Dr. Mary Blair, chair of stewardship at the Cathedral of the Incarnation in Baltimore, uses the image of the budget as the mortgage, and special projects as the pool. In order to have the pool, we need to fund the mortgage on the house. Refurnishing the pool might be more exciting, but unless the mortgage is paid, the pool can't function.

Although we have been very effective in promoting giving outside the budget, we have not been as effective in presenting the church's budget. Formerly, many congregations sent out a line item budget: clergy salary, gas and electric, secretary's salary, and diocesan (or denominational) requests, with a total amount needed to operate the church. People were then asked to fund the budget so there would not be a deficit.

We have learned that a "funding the budget" approach doesn't work; people don't give to a budget, but rather to mission and ministries. However, one always needs to have a proposed line item budget available for those few people who want to see it and for transparency.

The most effective way to present a budget is in the form of a narrative. In this type of budget, the rector's compensation is apportioned to worship (sermon preparation), pastoral care (hospital calls, counseling), administration (preparing the Sunday bulletin, vestry meetings), and outreach beyond the congregation (soup kitchen). Giving to the diocese, and through the diocese to the Episcopal Church, should be classified as outreach. A descriptive narrative of the category precedes the summary dollar amount. One of the most difficult tasks for the pastor is allocating their time to each of these ministries. I kept a monthly calendar and became aware how I was allocating my time each week.

Often the church creates a narrative budget for the fall stewardship program, but then puts it aside for the rest of the year. *One-Minute Stewardship: Creative Ways to Talk about Money in the Church* is an effective way to make the connection between a church member's weekly or monthly gift and the ministry that gift makes possible. Connecting people's contributions to the ministries of the church makes possible a conversation about our personal stewardship when we are not asking for money. There are many fine stewardship illustrations, and, as a rector, I found the most effective stewardship sermons were in the spring and summer when I was not asking congregants for more money. In fact, stewardship can be most effectively preached and taught in small doses, for example using four minutes of a twelve-minute homily.

C. Andrew Doyle, bishop of Texas, writes, "Our purpose is to have a conversation about stewardship which helps people connect their giving with their values, and their belief in a God who cares and helps people connect to one another."[1]

How Much Financial Support Should Someone Give to the Church?

In the Episcopal Church, the tithe is standard. The tithe is giving 10 percent of one's income for God's work. When I address this standard personally, I have found these particular organizations are where my heart is, and thus my treasure follows: The Cathedral of the Incarnation, Baltimore; The Episcopal Diocese of Maryland's Annual Ministry Appeal; The American Friends of the Episcopal Diocese of Jerusalem; Hobart College; Berkeley Divinity School at Yale; and then other charities. Each of you has those charities that speak to your passion.

In some denominations parishioners are asked to "give until it hurts." In the Episcopal Church, we have discovered Episcopalians have a very low pain threshold. I believe one should "give until it feels good." When one makes a Sunday offering, one's heart should glow with the ministries that the gift makes possible.

Some say no gift is too small. When you buy a gift for your family member, do you ask yourself, "What is the cheapest gift I can get away with?" Or do you think, "What gift can I afford that will truly make them happy and realize how much I love them?" When they open their gift and say, "You shouldn't have done this," how do you feel?

---

1. C. Andrew Doyle, *Church: A Generous Community Amplified for the Future* (Alexandria, VA: VTS Press, 2015), 190.

As I read the Gospels, "no gift too small" is not Jesus talking. If you believe no gift is too small, take your spouse or partner to a fast-food restaurant for your wedding anniversary. Choose to buy your child a package of bubble gum for their sixteenth birthday. Buy your mother a box of cake mix for Christmas. After one or more of these experiments, you will find out that indeed some gifts are too small.

At our cathedral we are undertaking a refurbishment of a hundred-year-old undercroft to be an attractive and large space for meetings and dinners. The request was made for funds, and I had planned to make a gift. One Sunday morning, in presenting this program, a speaker said, "No gift is too small." I took out one of the envelopes from the pew rack, wrote my name and "No gift is too small" on it. Then I placed a dollar bill in the envelope and the envelope in the offering plate. Just think, for only a dollar I could have my name listed as a donor and receive recognition for my gift. The dean was chagrinned when he saw my name listed as donating one dollar. I did it to prove a point: there are gifts that are too small. I subsequently made an appropriately sized gift for the undercroft renovation. The reception after my funeral (whenever that may be) will take place in the undercroft. I hope my family and friends can gather there to have lunch and celebrate my life by telling stories about me. I hope my legacy, besides my family, will be my having raised considerable money for God's work. I hope all the people with whom I have built relationships will remember, "No gift is too large for God's work."

The Rector's or Pastor's Role in Stewardship

The rector or pastor is the primary preacher and teacher of biblical stewardship. They present the principles of the stewardship message about God's abundant generosity. The pastor should not work alone, but with a dedicated stewardship committee or team to bring the stewardship message alive in the congregation. This committee should meet all year long and create a plan both for year-round stewardship and a plan for the fall stewardship campaign. In July or August, the vestry or governing board should approve plans for the fall campaign. The rector's or pastor's responsibility is always to be present when plans are made. However, it is not the pastor's role to run the meeting but to fully participate in the discussion and decision-making. This should be a team effort.

Stewardship is one of the congregation's most important committees. If there is a yearly diocesan stewardship conference, as many team members as possible should attend. If the rector or pastor goes alone and comes home with some good ideas, implementing them would be very difficult, if not impossible. But if committee members attended the same conference, they will implement some of the new ideas about stewardship that they heard.

My experience has taught me that with a good stewardship campaign, a good year will follow. The good year comes from having enough money to fund ministries and pay the bills. A weak stewardship campaign leads to poor pledging, and a difficult year follows. During a difficult year, vestry meetings must deal with budget cuts to the congregation's ministries. During a financial squeeze it often seems easy to say, "Let's cut the amount of money we send to the diocese." I have always fought this. What kind of example are we sending our pledgers if we cut the diocesan giving that funds ministries that we could not do by ourselves? When finances are tight, might not parishioners also see their contributions to the parish as expendable?

In summary, it takes a lot of hard work to have effective biblically based stewardship in your church. In my forty-eight years of experience, I have found no simple or easy answers. The energy and time the rector or pastor devotes to the church's stewardship effort pays off in the fulfilling of the church's ministries and mission.

I have one warning to rectors and pastors. Please don't rely on electronic requests when you solicit pledges from your congregation. Your parishioners make many credit card donations online to a variety of charities. At a Chesapeake Planned Giving Council meeting, I learned that over 60 percent of people who make online donations make them after they have received a letter asking for their gift. In many churches one can go online to make their pledge, but normally they are responding to a request they have received in "snail mail."

Should the Rector Know How Much a Church Member Gives?

The Rev. Charles LaFond says:

> Though it can be a touchy subject, it is best for the rector to know what people pledge and whether people pay their pledge. The rector need not worry that having this information will affect his or her relationships with members. Just as hearing confessions should not change a priest-parishioner relationship, neither should knowledge of pledge amounts change the pastoral relationship.[2]

As a young assistant, I was aware of what people gave to the congregation I served, and what they gave amazed me. Teachers sometimes gave more than well-paid executives. For example, I was giving four times more than a vice president of a prominent bank. I also saw the way token givers dealt with adversity. In 1969, the Episcopal General Convention passed a special program to deal with the racial unrest. The program was very controversial throughout the Episcopal Church. I saw our major givers lined up outside the rector's office to share their concern. Not one of those major givers cancelled their pledge. It was those who gave minimally of their income who cancelled their pledge in outrage. As a priest, parishioners have and shared their stories with me concerning adultery, drug and alcohol abuse, child abuse, and abortion. If I can't handle knowing how much parishioners give, should I be trusted with the intimate details of their lives? I believe it is crucial for the pastor to know how much their people are giving to further the mission of their congregation.

When I became rector of my first church, I asked the church secretary for the pledge records. I saw there were eight persons who were giving $1,000 a year, that is, $8,000 of $24,000 in pledged income. Not knowing the people, I asked the secretary their ages. She responded that

---

2. Charles LaFond, *Fearless Church Fundraising: The Practical and Spiritual Approach to Fundraising* (New York: Morehouse Publishing, 2012), 36.

seven of the eight were over sixty-five. I took this data, not the names, to the vestry and shared we had a serious problem in the future. We could work on our stewardship now or wait for the crisis. The vestry decided to work on the issue of giving now, and we were able to grow the financial resources to further God's mission.

During that time, I was trained as a consultant for the Alabama Plan, a disciplined way to conduct a stewardship campaign based on the tithe. I also learned about the concept of proportional giving. This approach treats giving as a percent of one's income. Givers should strive to increase the percent of their income each year that they give to God's work. I remember well one conversation in the kitchen of St. Matthew's Church. Eddie, a cook in the Navy, had just retired, and he shared he was keeping his pledge the same on less income, thus increasing his proportional giving to the church. He said it with a smile on his face.

I also learned it is hard to change a person's mind about the value of tithing. Sanford was the senior warden when I arrived at St. Matthew's. We became good friends. Some years later he shared with me, "With all this talk about tithing, people are now giving more, and the church is now more financially stable; I still don't like the idea of tithing."

When I arrived at my last parish, I inherited a structural deficit. Our pledge income did not meet the expenses of the congregation. The good news is we had some limited savings to make up the deficit. So we went to work with year-round stewardship, and in three years were able to have a balanced budget. When I preached my first stewardship sermon, a woman in the congregation responded that she did not like the church talking about money. She said she was cancelling her pledge and leaving the congregation. She took her five-dollar-a-week pledge and went elsewhere. I wished her well and was thankful I knew what people gave. I have found, as a pastor, that knowing what people gave in proportion to their resources helped me choose leadership in the congregation and evaluate their commitment to the congregation. One often finds the biggest complainers are token givers.

I also believe a pastor should witness to their own giving in context to their salary and housing allowance. As part of my stewardship sermon each fall I would say, "To support the mission and ministries of St. Thomas' Church, my wife and I will be pledging $_____ a week for the coming year." Leaders lead. In many congregations the clergy are among the highest givers. If a pastor knows what parishioners give, shouldn't the parishioners know how much the pastor gives? What the pastor gives shows how committed he or she is to the ministries of their church. I pledge $75.00 a week to my beloved Cathedral, and my total giving to all the ministries in the Cathedral in 2016 was $4,971. This represents 7.5 percent of my income. My total charitable donations in 2016 were $9,486, which represents 13.5 percent of my income.

I also checked the financial statements that went out quarterly to each household for a change in giving patterns, noting those seriously behind in their pledges. It would take me a few hours to list them. I then would spend a few evenings making phone calls to their homes to check up on them without talking directly about their giving. I found that when people can't give, they stop coming to church. Pledge records can be the best attendance records. I never would ask about their pledge or their giving, but just a friendly checking in call: "I have missed you at worship, is everything okay?" I uncovered many pastoral needs, such as the loss of a job, personal illness, family illness, a child's membership on a traveling soccer team that plays on Sunday mornings, being upset with something that happened at the church, or, I am sad to say, sometimes being upset with me. I could never have survived as a pastor for some eighteen years at my last parish if there was not a lot of forgiveness taking place. I believe you can't have a happy and loving family or healthy church without lots of forgiveness.

How Might a Person's Financial Contribution to the Church Be Increased?

I believe that giving to God's work should be based on the tithe, and proportional giving. The reality is most people can't increase their pledge to a tithe in one fell swoop, but they can attain that level of giving over time through giving an increased proportion of their financial resources each year.

One of the most effective ways to increase giving is to write a personal letter asking for each pledging household to consider increasing a pledge by a specific dollar amount. The least effective is asking for a percentage increase, because the parishioner will often compare the percent raise they got on their job with the percent increase the church is asking for: "I didn't get a 10 percent raise, asking me for a 10 percent increase in giving is crazy." Yet asking someone to consider an increase from $65.00 to $75.00 a week makes it seem doable, although it is a 15 percent increase. Asking for consideration of an increase of a monthly pledge from $200.00 to $225.00 is a 13 percent increase, but also seems reasonable and doable.

A second way I have found effective is a giving chart based on a household's present pledge. It is a one-page document with the first column the household's current pledge, the second column a suggested increased amount, then the third column suggesting an amount to support future growth. It is a full page with amounts from $5.00 to $200.00 for weekly giving and $200.00 to $2,000 for monthly giving. Both are only suggested ranges based on your congregation's weekly and monthly pledge. I present this as an illustration:

Weekly Pledge	to keep our parish strong	for the growth of our parish
15.00	16.00	18.00
20.00	22.00	24.00
30.00	33.00	36.00
65.00	71.00	77.00
Monthly Pledge		
90.00	98.00	106.00
150.00	163.00	177.00
350.00	381.00	413.00

This chart makes an increase of giving plausible and possible. I have based these figures on a 9 percent and 18 percent increase of giving. I found with this approach about 41 percent to 47 percent of our givers increased their giving year after year. What we were asking of them seemed doable.

One suggestion I have, based on a congregation's culture, is to list all who have made pledges for the coming year on the back of the program. It is a way of witnessing to the faith of those who have said yes to financially supporting the congregation. This list also makes the congregation aware of those who have said yes and encourages others to pledge as well. If this is done, there should be a place on the pledge card to indicate you want to remain anonymous. Always double check. Never publish the name of a donor who wants to be anonymous.

Following the receipt of the pledges, the rector needs to write a personal letter to each pledging household thanking them for their pledge. The most effective, of course, is a handwritten thank-you note. Writing these notes is one of the most effective uses of time for the rector. It will have an incredibly positive impact over time. It helps build relationships, the key to increased giving over time. Leaders lead! J. Clif Christopher states, "The rule in fund-raising is that people give to people and not to programs."[3]

I have experienced the powerful impact of a personal "ask" and personal thank-you note. When Bishop Sutton asked me to join his staff and take responsibility for his Bishop's Appeal, 34 clergy had made gifts to the Bishop's Appeal the year before. We made three changes in our approach. First, I wrote a personal note to ask every clergy in our diocese for their gift, then followed up with another note if necessary. Second, I wrote a personal note to each of them thanking them for their gift, and citing how they were making a difference or how their gift was helping to change the world. Third, we listed all givers to the Bishop's Appeal in our Convention booklet, both clergy and laity, so they would be publically thanked. We went from 34 clergy givers to 207 over the period of 7 years. I attribute this increase not to a better brochure, but a better personal relationship,

---

3. J. Clif Christopher, *Not Your Parents' Offering Plate: A New Vision for Financial Stewardship* (Nashville: Abingdon Press, 2008), 52.

request, and thank you. Today it is easy to text or e-mail a thank you. I totally approve of this, but it is no substitute for a personal note.

Also during these seven years I wrote a note to each newly ordained priest or deacon and to all clergy who transferred into the Diocese of Maryland, welcoming them and offering to take them to lunch. During the lunch, I welcomed them on behalf of the bishop, offered my assistance, and started building a personal relationship. In fact, in Baltimore's Little Italy, at Germono's restaurant, a plaque adorns the table where I usually sit. It says, "Father Charles's Luncheon Ministry."

What Are the Six Most Important Words in Stewardship Efforts?

Bishop Doyle writes, "We need to translate the idea that we don't just tell people to give once a month for twelve months, but we connect them to ministries and giving opportunities all year round. Yes, it is good to talk about stewardship."[4] When I address our diocesan convention each year, I emphasize the power of six words, "Thank you, thank you, thank you." I also add my mantra, "No gift is . . . ," and the convention answers, ". . . too large!"

Here is an apocryphal story about what can happen when the rector is not informed about special gifts or parishioners' gifts. Tom, a member of Holy Cross Church, received a bequest from a distant uncle for $140,000. Tom lived a simple lifestyle, so he decided to share his good fortune with groups that had positively influenced his life. He chose to give:

- $10,000 to the YMCA, where he was a member.
- $10,000 to the town library, where he borrowed books every week.
- $10,000 to the Boy Scouts—they changed his life as a young boy.
- $10,000 to Church of the Holy Cross, where he worshipped every Sunday.

---

4. Doyle, *Church*, 194.

Here's what he received in response:

- The YMCA director called and thanked him and invited him to come to see the new exercise equipment that they purchased to replace worn-out equipment so more members could work out.
- The head librarian wrote him a personal note, and invited him to come and see the new computers she bought so children who did not have access to a computer at home could come to the library to improve the computer skills so necessary for their future success.
- The Boy Scout leader contacted him to thank him and invited him to the Methodist church for a troop dinner, where he would be the guest of honor. He was shown the new tents with floors in them purchased with his gift.

However, the rector of Holy Cross Church never acknowledged his gift or thanked him. The treasurer believed the rector should not know what people give, even special gifts, because it might compromise his pastoral care. What do you think Tom feels now about his generous gifts?

How Can We Say "Thank You" to the People Who Have Given Gifts?

Following the passing of the peace, clergy in many congregations make announcements, welcome newcomers, and then say, quickly, "Walk in love, as Christ loves us and gave himself for us, an offering and a sacrifice to God" (Eph. 5:2).[5] The ushers then pass the offering plates. The offering is presented to the celebrant, elevated by the celebrant, and whisked off to a credence table or a counting room. An observer would not realize that this was a critical part of the liturgy.

Our Episcopal prayer book instructs: "Representatives of the congregation bring the people's offering of bread and wine, and money or

---

5. The Book of Common Prayer (New York: The Church Hymnal Corporation, 1979), 343. Hereafter referred to as BCP.

other gifts, to the deacon or celebrant. The people stand while the offerings are presented and placed on the Altar" (BCP, 361). Bringing all the people's gifts to be offered to God begins the liturgy of the Table.

In some congregations clergy may refer to the "collection" or "collection plates or baskets." As I travel the Diocese of Maryland, I have never heard of or been to a parish that has hired a collection agency to go after parishioners who have not fulfilled their pledges. Do you wonder why people may not pledge? Maybe the subconscious reference to collection agencies is at play. We are not taking a collection, but we are gathering an offering, freely given in thanksgiving for all of God's blessings.

I believe we are missing a wonderful opportunity at the time of the offering to thank our church members for their generosity for making possible the ministries of the congregation, their diocese, the Episcopal Church, and many other ministries. Thank you, thank you, thank you—you cannot say that too often.

Thanking parishioners can be done verbally at offertory, printed in the service leaflet, printed in the monthly newsletter, or mentioned in the weekly or monthly e-mails to the congregation. From then on, it is based on relationships and connections one makes. These relationships and connections are based on meeting with people one-on-one and discovering people's passions. When I worked for Bishop Sutton in our Bishop's Appeal, I found I could get virtually anyone to give me $25.00 to shut me up. But if I wanted a generous gift, I needed to find their passion and connect their passion to a diocesan or parish ministry.

Our offertory gives us the perfect opportunity to thank our parishioners for the ministries they perform and those made possible through their offerings. Our parishioners need to be reminded that their pledge and offerings will help change lives and make a difference in our world for which Jesus Christ gave his life. We also need to be reminded of the abundance of God's blessings. We thank our parishioners for their generosity given from their abundance. The gathering of the offering gives the celebrant the opportunity weekly to say "thank you" and to acknowledge the good that is being done in the name of Christ with their offering.

Too often the offertory becomes a request for more money and not an appreciation of what they have given and are giving.

I want my parishioners to feel good as we gather and bless the offering. The offering plates or baskets placed on the altar represent our commitment to the ministries of the parish. Remember, that money could be used for dinners out, a new TV, paying down a credit card, taking a wonderful European vacation. Remember too that your parishioners' money can be given to many other worthy secular non-profits. Giving to your congregation is a decision that can change if the giver does not believe that the offering they make is being used for God's work.

J. Clif Christopher states, "People want to make the world a better place to live. They want to believe that they can truly make a difference for the better. There is embedded in us, it seems, a desire to finish out our work on this earth with a sense that we amounted to something. To sum it up, people want to be part of something that *changes lives*."[6]

One summer I had the privilege of being the celebrant at the Cathedral of the Incarnation, where I worship when I am was not traveling through the diocese preaching on stewardship and planned giving. The men of the choir led us in music and did a fine job. At the time of the offering following announcements, I shared this with the congregation, "I want to thank the men of our choir for coming together to lead our worship this morning. I also want to thank our organist and choir director, Ken Brown, for his wonderful leadership Sunday by Sunday. I especially want to thank the members of the Cathedral for your pledges and offerings that support our fine music program. When you hear a moving anthem, you helped to make it possible. Remember that no gift is too large for God's work here at our Cathedral." Ken and the choir members had big smiles on their faces as we acknowledged their ministry, and the congregation was grateful their offerings were acknowledged.

---

6. Christopher, *Not Your Parents' Offering Plate*, 13.

How Do We Say "Thank You" to God and How Does God Respond?

In the Episcopal Church we gather for the Holy Eucharist; in other denominations the meal is called Holy Communion or the Lord's Supper. In the prayer book it is called the Great Thanksgiving, because it is truly God's great generosity and blessing to us for which we are giving thanks. The word "Thanksgiving" is a combination of "thanks" and "giving." Both are keys to a healthy spiritual life. If we as a congregation were to combine all our personal assets—bank accounts, IRAs, 401ks, home equity—it would be inadequate to purchase Holy Communion. Sunday by Sunday, we increase our faith by sharing the Eucharist. Everyone is welcome; come as you are. Parishioners on any given Sunday are happy, sad, hopeful, dealing with cancer in their family, celebrating a son or daughter getting accepted to college, or another flunking out. In the Episcopal Church, if you didn't come to worship, there would be no Eucharist celebrated, because an Episcopal priest or bishop can't celebrate communion alone.

In many evangelical churches, there is an altar call. The pastor invites all who want to accept Jesus to come forward and be prayed for. In the Episcopal, Lutheran, Methodist, and Roman Catholic denominations, the priest or pastor holds up the paten and chalice—the bread and wine—speaks the words of invitation, and everyone is invited to come. The parishioner must make a decision to come forward and accept Jesus. In some traditions people accept the bread and wine in remembrance of Jesus's sacrifice on the Cross. In other traditions, priest and people understand the Real Presence of Christ is in the consecrated bread and the wine. They come forward to receive the bread and wine as Christ's body and blood.

When one leaves the church after receiving communion, one leaves as a new person, filled again with Jesus Christ. In my imagination, I would love to have a means of seeing all my parishioners, say on a Tuesday afternoon. In this vision I could see where Jesus was, for they are the hands and feet of Christ. They are practicing their stewardship, wherever they are.

The Eucharist is a gift from God purchased by Jesus Christ's freely offered sacrifice on the Cross for us. When you are feeling down or depressed, feeling alone after a tough day, and wondering if God really loves you, in your mind's eye imagine the Cross and think of Jesus hanging there. The answer you should receive to the question about whether God loves you: a resounding YES!

Ultimate Stewardship: Don't Leave a Mess

I am known as the "grim preacher" in the Episcopal Diocese of Maryland; you will soon know why. Remember that there is a 100 percent mortality rate among everyone who reads this book. But as Christians, we don't need to worry or be anxious about death. We have been given the promise of eternal life. We know where we are going. At age seventy-five, I tell my family I am ready, but in no hurry, for none of us knows the time or the hour of our death. In the planning for the end of my life I have a mantra: "Don't leave a mess."

The most dangerous thing many of us do each day is commute to work. Every week, good people die on the highway. If this happens to you, would your family say, "They had everything organized." Or would they say, "What a mess they left!"

I want to share four things that concern how you wish things to happen after you die. The Episcopal Church Foundation has a wonderful booklet called "Planning for the End of Life: Faithful Stewards of Your Good Gifts" that contains a medical directive and various instructional documents for a health proxy, forms for planning your funeral, and various documents to assist you in preparing to write your will. It can be purchased in quantity for your parish from Forward Movement Publications or downloaded from ECF's website. The documents provided are not intended to be legal documents but a workbook to help you review your wishes so that you can take the next steps in working with appropriate professional advisors to finalize your plans.

Medical Directive

First, each person should have a medical directive, designating a person to make decisions for you when you are unable to make them for yourself. You will decide whether you want extraordinary procedures, like a feeding tube, when there is no hope of recovery. Every state offers one for you, and you should contact or download from your state the appropriate documents for where you live. An attorney may not even be necessary. None of us wants our medical decisions made by a court or by others who do not know your wishes.

When you complete your medical directive, give copies to your doctor and family members. Discuss your wishes with those whom you have chosen to make medical decisions when you are not able to do so and with your family. The time for this discussion is not when you are in intensive care and a decision must be made about whether to continue care for you. It needs to be made when you are healthy and can express what you desire for yourself.

Whom will you choose to make these decisions when you are unable to? You might find one of your children says, "I could never make this decision; I would feel terrible the rest of my life," while the other says, "I have seen enough people needlessly suffer at the end of their life, so I would be able to follow out your wishes." It may become quite clear which person you should choose.

Planning Your Funeral

Second, each person should consider making plans for your funeral. A plan for your funeral would answer questions such as these:

- Do you want a church service with Holy Communion?
- Would you like just a burial service in a funeral home of your choosing?

- Do you want to be cremated? Do you want to buried in a casket?
- Do you want to have calling hours?
- Do you want an open or closed casket?
- What are your favorite scriptures and hymns?
- Do you want flowers or, in lieu of flowers, gifts given in your memory to your church or favorite charity?

It is important to discuss your funeral plans with your spouse, children, or loved ones. None of us want family conflict at the time of our death. None of us want to leave a mess.

Creating a Last Will and Testament

Third, do you have a will? Is your will up-to-date? This is a trick question. Everyone reading this book has a will. You may have one that you thoughtfully prepared (often with the help of an attorney), designating how you want to have your estate distributed after you have entered eternal life. If you have not created a will or a trust, your state will specify what will happen to your assets. To ensure that your wishes will be fulfilled, I encourage you to seek appropriate professional legal assistance in finalizing your will and/or trust.

Our practice as Christians should be to make plans after our death for the care of loved ones and to support worthy causes. The Episcopal Church's Book of Common Prayer states, "The minister of the Congregation is directed to instruct the people, from time to time, about the duty of Christian parents to make prudent provision for the well-being of their families, and for all persons to make wills, while they are in good health, arranging for the disposal of their temporal goods, not neglecting, if they are able, to leave bequests for religious and charitable uses." (BCP, 445).

It may surprise you that this admonition does not accompany the directions of the burial rite. In fact, it is too late to have it there. It is found, though, in the worship service entitled "A Thanksgiving for the Birth or Adoption of a Child." In particular, the Episcopal Church believes parents need wills to provide for their child or children in the case of their death.

Writing a Will Based on One's Family Life

- If you are single, will you plan to make bequests to your parents, siblings, nieces, and/or nephews? What about including your college, your church, and/or your favorite charities?
- When you marry, you will most likely make your spouse your only beneficiary. But one always needs to have contingent beneficiaries in case both spouses were to die together under such tragic circumstances as an automobile accident, a house fire, or an epidemic. These contingent beneficiaries could also include charities.
- If you have young children, all your resources will be needed for your spouse to raise and care for your children. Contingent beneficiaries would only come into play in case of a tragedy which had caused the death of the entire family.
- However, when your children are grown and on their own, many spouses choose to have reciprocal wills or trust agreements. All assets go to the surviving spouse, but on his or her death, bequests pass directly to their children, to their church, and/or to other charities.

However, there are some instances where your family does not need all your treasure. Here are some examples from my last parish where I served for eighteen years (St. Thomas' in Towson, Maryland). I have changed the first names to protect the person's and families' privacy.

George came to me and shared he was tithing 10 percent of his estate after he and his wife had entered eternal life. He had four children; each would receive 22.5 percent of his estate rather than 25 percent of his estate. He said it would not make a real difference to them, but he felt it would make a real difference to St. Thomas'. In addition, their bequest would provide a witness to others about how important St. Thomas' was in his family's life.

Carol came to me. She had remembered St. Thomas' in her will. She was divorced and had no children. When she was sick, parishioners brought food to her home and clergy brought her communion. St. Thomas' was her family, and she wished to express her gratitude.

Gladys was divorced and had one daughter. She shared with me that she was leaving $14,000 in her will to the Outreach Fund of St. Thomas'.

As her legacy, she wanted her parish to have greater resources to reach out to those in need.

More Reasons to Create a Will

Each person needs his or her own will. No one wants family members to pay for unneeded legal and other expenses when a will does not exist. When I preach and teach in the Diocese of Maryland, I propose three scenarios to explain why it is important to avoid leaving a mess for your heirs to clean up. Here are the three scenarios when someone dies without a will:

1. A couple is married and has two children, ages 14 and 16. One spouse dies. What happens to non–jointly owned property?
2. A couple is married, perhaps for five years, perhaps for thirty years. There are no children. One spouse dies. Who gets the non–jointly owned property?
3. A couple is married and has two adult children and two adult step-children. All the children are financially independent. One spouse dies. Who gets the non–jointly owned property?

The following outcomes are based on the state of Maryland's will for someone who dies without a personal will. Most people who have heard my sermon or who have participated in a seminar I taught are shocked about these outcomes:

1. His or her estate is divided, one-half to the husband or wife and one-half to the two children, 25 percent each. Their money is kept in trust for them, and when they reach the age of eighteen, they receive their inheritance with no guidance. If both parents were to die at the same time, the children would receive 50 percent of the estate again at age eighteen with no guidance. Could you have managed a significant estate at age eighteen? When you are eighteen and have plenty of money, you have plenty of friends.
2. The surviving spouse would receive 50 percent of the estate, and the parents of the deceased would receive 50 percent even if they had

abused the deceased and did all in their power to destroy the marriage. If both parents are deceased, then the entire estate would go to the surviving spouse.

3. The surviving spouse would receive the first $15,000 of the estate. Then the remainder of the estate would be divided with 50 percent going to the surviving spouse and 50 percent divided between biological children. The step-children would receive nothing.

My Personal Choices

Thankfully, my wife and I had our own wills. If I had died before my wife, 100 percent of my estate would have gone to my wife. Nothing was left to my two children or to my two stepchildren, all of whom are financially independent.

Things did not go as we had expected. But when my beloved wife, Judy, died of multiple myeloma in January 2014, both our wills and estate plans were up-to-date. It cost me only $7.80 to settle her estate in Maryland. There were no unnecessary legal expenses.

As I preach in the Diocese of Maryland, I share my will as a witness. When God calls me home, my four children (two biological children and two stepchildren, all of whom call me "Dad") will each receive 20 percent of my estate. Twenty percent will be left for charitable work.

Even though I struggled in college and graduated with a C average, Hobart College prepared me for a life of consequence; it will receive 5 percent. Berkeley Divinity School at Yale provided the spiritual formation I needed to serve Jesus for some forty-seven years as a parish priest. Berkeley will receive 5 percent. I served for four years as president of the American Friends of the Episcopal Diocese of Jerusalem (AFEDJ). This diocese struggles daily to serve people with dire needs. In support of its efforts to aid that diocese, AFEDJ will receive 5 percent. I served eighteen years as rector of St. Thomas' Church, Towson, Maryland. They were kind to me and cared for my wife and for me. They will receive 5 percent.

Why have I used percentages? No one knows what one's worth will be at death. Your home might be worth twice what it is now or half of what it is worth now. The value of investments may rise or fall. Percentages make it fair to everyone.

You should also remember your estate can be worth significantly more than what your will covers. Your estate may include your life insurance policies, IRAs, a 401k, a 403b. The assets from these instruments will be distributed by beneficiary designations rather than by your will.

When I teach about creating a plan to distribute one's assets, I tell people how easy it is to remember one's church and/or favorite charities by designating them as beneficiaries of an IRA or 401k, or other accounts which can be designated to pay to a beneficiary on death. Just call up the institution holding those assets and they will send you a form. Fill it out remembering the church and your favorite charities, and it is done. No lawyer, no expense.

Isn't Estate Planning Only for the Wealthy?

The Diocese of Maryland has an All Saints Legacy Society. It now includes 483 households. They have remembered their parish, the Diocese of Maryland, or the Bishop Claggett Conference Center in their will/estate plans. In an address to the 2017 Diocese of Maryland convention, I shared with the convention delegates that the All Saints Legacy Society includes 43 clergy, who are not generally known to be wealthy! I heard a lot of laughter.

Bishop Eugene Taylor Sutton followed my presentation by witnessing to his own will/estate plans. Following his death and that of his beloved wife, Sonya, he will remember his four children with 80 percent of his estate and the church for the other 20 percent. Leaders lead by example!

In the Diocese of Maryland, all the members of the All Saints Legacy Society receive a printed invitation enclosed in a hand-addressed envelope, inviting them to be recognized by our bishop at a special service on a Sunday afternoon. They receive a Diocesan Legacy Society pin. A reception in the bishop's house follows. Members come from both small and large congregations.

Bishop Sutton believes that the way to build a strong diocese is by building strong parishes. When I share this with clergy, no one has disagreed. Our diocesan staff is committed to strengthening our congregations. I believe that most of those in our Diocesan Legacy Society have remembered only their congregation in their estate plans. Others, however, including many clergy, have remembered the diocese and Bishop Claggett Center, Seafarers Center, and parish schools as well. Many of us reading this book will be able to remember our parish, diocese, or conference center in our estate plans.

Episcopalians have a wonderful resource in the Episcopal Church Foundation. They have a comprehensive toolkit called *Planned Giving on Demand,* which includes numerous resources, including webinars, online articles, and a useful book called *Funding Future Ministry: A Guide to Planned Giving.* This book is one that every congregation small and large should possess. Plus, they offer many brochures and booklets that cover charitable gift annuities, charitable remainder trusts, pooled income fund, *Planned Giving: Stewards of God's Bounty,* and of course the booklet I described earlier, *Planning for the End of Life: Faithful Stewards of God's Gifts.* These can all be ordered through the Episcopal Church Foundation. The Episcopal Church Foundation stands ready to help you institute a Planned Giving Program in your Congregation. Not an Episcopalian? Check with your denomination's headquarters and I am sure they will be able and happy to assist your congregation.

The Three Testaments

When I preach my "Don't Leave a Mess" sermon, I talk about the "three testaments." First, the Old Testament, called the Hebrew Bible, tells the creation story and contains The Law, prophetic literature, and wisdom literature. Second, the New Testament, called the Christian Bible, tells about the birth of Jesus, his ministry, crucifixion, and resurrection. It contains accounts of the early church and letters written to various churches in the first century.

But there is a third testament, called "Your Last Will and Testament." When your family and loved ones read this after your death, it will serve as a testament to your life and your values. Who and what did you care about? What were you thankful for: your spouse and family members? your church? your college? the YMCA? the symphony? the Humane Society?

Let me end by sharing the story of Roberta. I always arrived at St. Thomas' at 6:30 on Sunday morning to practice my sermon out loud before I preached at the 8:00 Eucharist. Quite often Roberta would arrive about 6:45 as I was winding down my sermon. After I finished, I would sit down with her and have a conversation, since we were the only ones at the church. Over the years she shared with me how she came to St. Thomas' as a widow with her two children. She taught in the church school. She saw her students and her own children be confirmed, graduate from high school and college and move out of state. She was in her early eighties, lived in subsidized church housing, and worked as a companion. She would proclaim, "I take care of the elderly," emphasizing the word "elderly." She would go to their home at about 10 in the morning. She would visit with her charge, cook lunch, play cards, write notes, and leave to come home at about 4 in the afternoon. After work, the elderly person's children would arrive home, knowing their parent had been cared for.

Roberta only missed church when she visited her two children, and she would always let me know. Then she missed two Sundays. I felt concerned, so I called her home. There was no response. I called our local hospitals and found her at St. Joseph's. I immediately went and visited her. Roberta told me she was diagnosed with a brain tumor. There in her hospital room she shared with me her love of St. Thomas' and how important her church was to her and her children. She told me she had little in the way of material possessions. Her car was old and on its last legs. In fact, I once blessed her car to keep it on the road. She had two items of value: a gold watch her husband had given her when they were married and a ring that her father, a seafarer, had brought back from the Orient. She said she wanted to give them to St. Thomas' in thanksgiving for the parish. Her brain tumor was fast-growing, and she died in about two weeks. We held her burial service with Eucharist at St. Thomas', and then I buried her next to her husband. Two days later, her son came to my office at the church and presented me with the watch and ring. He explained how much he appreciated the care St. Thomas' had given his mother. An officer of the governing body of St. Thomas' and I took the watch and ring to a local jewelry store to be appraised. We sold the watch. I bought Roberta's ring from St. Thomas' so I could show it when I told her story. The money went into St. Thomas' Heritage Fund to help the church meet the needs of future generations.

As I reflect on this story, a question comes to mind. Roberta showed her love for St. Thomas' by her words and through her bequest. Would you show love for your church in the same way? You, too, can make a difference.

How to Construct Your Own Stewardship Meditations and Use Them to Encourage Generous Giving

The meditations in this book are designed to inspire your church to be one that appreciates all who give their time, talents and abilities, and money. Their generosity makes it possible for your church to realize its mission, through the ministries of your congregation. The meditations can be memorized, or just rewritten to make them appropriate for your congregation. Buy this book for yourself. Also give it to each member of your clergy team, stewardship committee, vestry, and person responsible for your communications to the congregation, and then ask them to read it as their homework. Tell them it is their copy, mark it up. Check off the meditations they like on giving (G), stewardship (S), special occasions (SO), and planned giving (P).

Then gather them all together, not during the stewardship season, but in the winter, spring, or summer for a joint stewardship committee and vestry meeting, along with the communication people. Ask them to list and discuss the ministries that are making a difference. By engaging in these ministries, your church members give their time, talents and abilities, and money to your congregation, to your community, to the diocese, and to the Episcopal Church. This will be an enlightening and positive exercise.

Take the list and plan out the year, such as using a meditation for the opening of church school, at the time of food in-gathering, for Godly Play teachers, for hospitality hour hosts, for hospital visitors, for Boy/Girl Scouts, for the Legacy Society, the altar guild, for adult and/or children's choir members, for the worship planning team. Special work at the diocesan level also can receive thankful attention, such as youth ministry, or planning for the bishop's visitation. Finally, there are ministries of the entire Episcopal Church that can be recognized and thanked, such as Episcopal Relief and Development, Episcopal Migration Ministries, and even being part of the Jesus Movement. Again, the purpose of this exercise is to connect these ministries with church members' stewardship.

Then check off these ministries against the mediations from this book. Decide which ones you would like to use as is, which ones you would like to rewrite, and which ones you want to compose from scratch. Pick out the meditations you want to share with the congregation in order to educate them and help them grow in their understanding of stewardship. At the time of the offering, the members of your congregation should be encouraged to feel good about the money they put in the offering plate, as well as the money deducted from their checking account by EFT, or the money given through an IRA distribution. They will feel good about their giving because of the wonderful ministries being done in their name. They will appreciate being thanked for giving their time, their talents and abilities, and their money. Over time, this feeling of being appreciated will result in more generous giving.

Below is a simple outline to organize what your gathering may decide to highlight for each month of the year, but one does not have to wait for January, one can begin at any month.

January:	Feast of the Epiphany	S9	P 47
	Acolytes	SO1	P 89
February:	Lent 1/Episcopal Relief and Development Sunday	SO34	P 110

	Boy Scouts	SO11	P 95
March:	Adult Choir	SO2	P 90
	All Is Gift	G1	P 71
April:	Palm Sunday	S22	P 57
	Legacy Society—Parish	SO59	P 132
May:	Hospitality	SO55	P 127
	Generous Living	S13	P 50
June:	Church School—End of Year	SO20	P 101
	Episcopal Migration Ministries/ Refuge Day, June 20th	SO29	P 106
July:	Consider Your Heavens	SO22	P 102
	Giving and Receiving Dignity	G7	P 76
August:	Facebook	SO38	P 114
	Gratitude for the Community of Faith	SO49	P 122
September:	Church School	SO19	P 100
	"Firstness"	G3	P 73
October:	Godly Play—Parable of the Good Samaritan	SO47	P 121
	Greeters	SO50	P 123
November:	Baptism—All Saints' Day	SO8	P 93
	Veterans Day—We Are the Stewards of Everything	SO73	P 143
December:	St. Nicholas of Myra at Christmastide—December 6th	SO69	P 140
	Gift of Shoes	G6	P 75

Section IV

Stewardship Meditations

Armistice Day

On the eleventh day of the eleventh month, Remembrance Day in Britain (Veteran's Day in the United States), people remember the sacrifice of others in two terrible world wars. Ten years ago on Remembrance Day I stood, at midnight, at the high altar of London's Westminster Abbey. I was attending a dinner in the Jerusalem Chamber adjoining the Abbey and, late in the proceedings, I noticed a half-opened door, slipped through, and found myself alone in that spectacular monument to faith, hope, and love. I wandered the aisles, visited the side chapels, reflected beside the blanket of scarlet poppies that covered the national war memorial, and stood before the ancient high altar. And in that profound stillness, it dawned on me: all that splendor, all that soaring stone and radiant glass, all those tombs of the great and the good, that entire glorious place was one vast offering—an offering of thanks to God for beauty, for courage, for intellect and imagination, for love, a love that led generations of saints to lay down their lives for others. I realized that that is what we are here for: to recognize the very best that is in us and then raise it high, offering it in joyful gratitude to God, the source and goal of everything that is and ever can be. That is what we are here for.

If we can begin to wean our needy selves from get and grab and gain and move toward caring, sharing, giving, then we will learn the glorious secret of that vast and holy place. Then we will begin at last to live the life we were created for, the life that Jesus came to open up for us again. Then we will finally grasp what Saint Paul meant when he spoke of "possessing all things in Christ."

The Rev. Dr. J. Barrie Shepherd
Minister Emeritus of historic First Presbyterian Church,
New York, New York

Blessing of Time   S 2

In seminary, I was called to the office by the dean and told he was sending me to the home of a widow to go through her husband's clothes as part of my role as president of the class and my work study. Her husband had died about a year earlier and she finally felt it was time to begin giving away his clothes. I was not happy. I had better things to do. I protested. He insisted. I went. When I arrived, she took me into this large walk-in closet and began slowly pulling out items of clothing. With each one she would tell me a bit about a moment or a memory that went with that article of clothing. We did this for hours. When we got to the very end, she pulled out a beautiful long winter coat that was obviously hand tailored. She held it for a long time, and then looked at me and said, "I think this would fit you. This was his favorite winter coat. I want you to have it." It fit perfectly. Some twenty years later, it is still my favorite winter coat. Stapled on the inside coat pocket, as is often done at dry cleaners, was his last name. The label is still there, as a reminder of a true day of blessings, when I met this man though his wife's memories. We are stewards of everything God has given to us, and time is one very important gift which we are called to nurture and to care for. I thought the task would be wasted time; instead it was one of the greatest blessings I have ever received. Listen. Watch. Be Open.

The Rt. Rev. Gregory H. Rickel
Bishop, Diocese of Olympia

Called to Be Stewards   S 3

God's generous creation has a wonderful and grand moment of consummation: the creation of humankind. The very culmination of creation is that of humanity made in the image and likeness of God. We have been created in goodness as God's daughters and sons with a striking resemblance to our Creator, the divine imprint within our identity and nature.

The Genesis story moves quickly from our human creation and identity to our responsibility. "Be fruitful and multiply, and fill the earth." Generosity becomes generative action on our part. The human response to the generosity of God is to be generous in return. What is encouraged here is stewardship—our use and shaping of the gifts of creation around us in ways to serve the humanity and the earth itself. We are called to be stewards of God's gifts, reflecting the same generosity and love that God has shown to us.

Remember, you are created in the very image of God, and you bear the family resemblance of God. You have been given gifts of intelligence and creativity, of relationship and provision. You are precious, wondrously good and deeply loved. You have also been given the responsibility to be a steward of the gifts given to you.

Have you looked in a mirror lately? I don't mean the one on your wall at home. Rather, I mean the one of your heart and soul. Have you looked at your image, your likeness, to behold what a marvelous and loved creature you are? Have you seen that you bear resemblance to your Creator? Have you looked at the gifts that God has given you? Will you take stock of them and see how strong and abundant they are? How are you using them?

The Rev. Dr. James B. Lemler
Rector, Christ Church, Greenwich, Connecticut

Clean Heart   S 4

Psalm 51:1–13, Lent 5B and Proper 13B

Our Psalm reading petitions God to create in us a clean heart. We hear this at the beginning of every Holy Eucharist when we pray, "Almighty

God, to you all hearts are open, all desires known, and from you no secrets are hid; Cleanse the thoughts of our hearts by the inspiration of your Holy Spirit, that we may perfectly love you, and worthily magnify your holy Name; through Christ our Lord. Amen" (BCP, 355).

Invite this petition to resonate and pulse deeply within. Pray for your heart to be filled with the Holy Spirit and opened to God, and also for your heart to know and embrace openness of every sort. Open your heart to God and to your neighbor. Dwell in the openness of a heart broken open. Abide in a church that opens its doors widely so those on the inside go out into the world, those out in the world are warmly invited in, and the windows of all our souls are flung wide open to exchange our light. Open your heart to the wonder and mystery of God. And breathe deeply so that your heart is indeed open to yourself. Know, claim, and share all the wondrous gifts God generously gives.

Julie Simonton
Officer for Congregational Development and Stewardship,
The Episcopal Diocese of Virginia

Created for Good   S 5

"In the beginning when God created the heavens and the earth. . . ." That's how Genesis begins, a good place to start in any reflection about stewardship. This is the beginning word, the first word, a proclamation of generosity and goodness. God generously created life and light on that first day. There are other days to follow and more to come. And all of it is good. The Hebrew word *tov* (good) is pronounced by God at the end of each creative act. How amazing to think that God could be so generous in creating everything needed for life and the universe. The poetry is meant to be read as a paean of praise, not a scientific text. It finds its expression as we voice praise to God in our hearts.

Scripture describes a consummately generous God, a God who doesn't hold back. God is extravagant in gifts and in love. *Tov*: it is all so very, very good. The same generous creativity of God sustains us in our lives now. Our life of faith is to recognize the creative good that God has given to the world and to us, not to take it for granted.

"In the beginning" was creation, goodness, generosity. It was true for the universe and for human life itself. It is true right now for your life and for mine. God gave us a beginning. God gives new beginnings, too. This very moment can be such a time of new beginning. Stop for a moment. Take stock of your life and your faith. Where do you see the good? Where do you witness the creation anew? How might you have a new beginning right now, at this time? "It is good. . . ." God is good.

The Rev. Dr. James B. Lemler
Rector, Christ Church, Greenwich, Connecticut

Discernment and Chocolate S 6

I have often been asked what will turn the tide in stewardship in our country. I guess because I write books and blogs on the subject, people turn to me when they want more money from their people for their budgets. It makes sense, I guess. I generally tell them that the best way to raise money in a congregation is to buy them each a candle and teach them how to pray. I get annoyed looks. It happens a lot.

Churches want better pledge cards, more parties, more creative kick-off events, and nicer signage so that people will give more. They want to be impressive and attract confidence and thereby money. And sometimes it works. It can be creepy, but it works. The deeper question for a church is, do you really deserve the money you seek to raise? Would Jesus make the stewardship speech at your campaign dinner, or would he flip over the tables and use naughty words?

Sitting silently with a candle in the darkness of a morning is harder than one would think. To do so, one is faced with one's self and with one's God. If you believe in an angry God, then it is even harder. Alone with a candle, one is faced with the accomplishments and failures of the previous day. One smells one's stinky heart bits. Alone with a candle one is faced with a savior whose radical life-choices make us uncomfortable. What do we do with a Jesus who chose poverty and gave himself away?

Alone with a candle, God can whisper to us that we are loved. We don't want to hear that. We want to hear we will be rich enough to never be vulnerable. Alone with a candle we are not rushing around self-anesthetizing against our fears and griefs. If we fill our days, our lives, even our worship with enough stuff to do, then we won't actually have to sit and listen—to our hearts, to our conscience, to our God. We won't be able to hear hard questions about how our lives square with the kind of God we say we worship. Do we follow Jesus or are we simply members of a church? I could go to a weekly meeting about Willie Wonka without having the meetings much change my life—though the chocolate after the meetings would be a draw. I love chocolate.

The Rev. Canon Charles LaFond
Canon Steward, Saint John's Cathedral, Denver, Colorado

Eagerly Presenting Our Offerings   S 7

The apostle Paul said, "For if the eagerness is there, the gift is acceptable according to what one has—not according to what one does not have" (2 Cor. 8:12). As we prepare to worship our Lord through giving, let us display our eagerness in response to how the Lord has blessed us. Let us eagerly present our tithes and offerings, as we work to support the building of God's kingdom.

The Rev. Melvin Amerson
The Methodist Foundation, Austin, Texas

Faithful Servant—Doing What Is Right   S 8

When we talk of stewardship, our thoughts normally turn to money. However, while our giving to support the church is an important part of being good stewards, it isn't the whole thing. Faithful stewards are servants and they clearly understand two things. First of all, they know whom they serve; secondly, their loyalty is not for sale, not even to the one whom they serve. The Roman writer Plutarch tells a story about King Antipater and his advisor Phocion: "As Phocion, therefore, answered

King Antipater, who sought his approbation of some unworthy action, 'I cannot be a flatterer and your friend.' "[1]

In Jeremiah we find a similar story of loyalty by a servant of King Zedekiah (Jer. 38:1–13). Zedekiah, frequently troubled by the prophet Jeremiah, abdicated his responsibility and told some of his advisors to do what they wanted with Jeremiah. They threw Jeremiah in a cistern, and left him there to die. But Zedekiah had a faithful servant named Ebed-Melech (a name that literally means "servant of the king") who informed the king that his counselors, acting in his name, had acted wickedly, and that if the king did not do something, the prophet would die. The king wisely had the servant pull Jeremiah out of the cistern.

Isaiah wrote four songs about the "Servant of God." In his first song (Isa. 42:1–3) we learn that the servant's, or steward's, ultimate concern is with justice being done. In both Hebrew and Greek the same word is used for "justice" and "righteousness." Doing what is just is doing what is right, and certainly faithful stewards will strive to do what is right and just.

The Rev. Fred Weimert
Vice President of the Board,
Central Maryland Ecumenical Council

Feast of the Epiphany S 9

Matthew 2:1–12

Giving is an act of worship. In fact, it was the very first act of worship. On that inaugural Feast of the Epiphany, the Magi were filled with overwhelming joy at finding the Christ child. They fell down on their faces and knees, recognizing him as king and savior, and presenting to him the gifts of gold, frankincense, and myrrh. Over time all sorts of

---

1. Plutarch, "Agis," in *The Lives of the Noble Grecians and Romans, Great Books of the Western World,* ed. Robert Maynard Hutchins (Chicago: Encyclopedia Britannica, 1952), 14:649.

symbolic meaning has been attached to these three gifts. Gold indicates royalty and recognizes the Christ child as the newborn king—a king for every nation who draws people together. Frankincense, a type of incense, was burned in houses of worship as an offering intended to please God. This gift recognizes the divinity of Jesus. And myrrh was an embalming spice, an ointment used to prepare bodies for burial. This gift recognizes the human nature of Christ and foretold of his suffering and death.

But there is another important element to these three iconic gifts. Scholars also point out that gold, frankincense, and myrrh were tools of the Magi's trade—they were items that these wise men would have had sitting around in their offices. Myrrh-ink, in particular, was used daily in writing down magical charms and their foretellings. The wise men brought to Jesus, as gifts, products of their own countries and labor. Their gifts were directly related to their own everyday work. They brought what they had—not what they didn't have. Have you ever toyed with this question of what gift you would bring to the Christ child? What could ever be good enough? The Epiphany story teaches us that we are called to bring ourselves to God. Our very own treasures and talents. True worship indeed.

The Rev. Suzanne M. Culhane
Canon for Stewardship, Diocese of Long Island

Finding Treasures   S 10

"Do not store up for yourselves treasures on earth, where moth and rust consume and where thieves break in and steal; but store up for yourselves treasures in heaven." (Matt. 6:19–20)

Where are your treasures? What are your treasures? These are probing questions for us all. Jesus taught his followers about discipleship. He taught about the fullness and hope of life itself. He asks about treasures, not necessarily the kind that we lock away in safe deposit boxes and great chests. No, these are treasures locked away in our hearts.

What do we hold dear and precious in our own hearts? What do we value most in our lives? Jesus identifies a danger in passing, ephemeral, and illusory treasures, all that moth and rust consume, and as for security systems—they are hacked; thieves do break in and steal. We attach greater value to things than they are worth. Jesus knows that all that glitters is not gold. He suggests treasures that will endure: generosity, compassion, service, and deep care—precious, valuable treasures—and then asks us where our hearts are. That's the primary issue. "Where your treasure is, there your heart will be also." It's true. The things we hold precious—the treasures of our lives—are squarely where our hearts' love and desire are found. Jesus knows that God has truly magnificent and enduring treasures for us, if we will recognize and accept them.

Where are your treasures? What are your treasures? Consider these questions. Accept the treasures of God in your life. See through the short-lived and illusory ones. Where is your heart? Whom or what do you love and value? Whom or what do you hold dear? Let your heart experience the good, the beautiful, the enduring treasures of God today.

The Rev. Dr. James B. Lemler
Rector, Christ Church, Greenwich, Connecticut

Freely Give   S 11

"Thanks be to God for his indescribable gift!" (2 Cor. 9:15) powerfully acknowledges the sovereignty of God by the Apostle Paul. God's generosity flows out of God's gift of grace. Something described as "indescribable" often points to an action or object so awesome that few words can adequately describe or explain it. Now we have the opportunity to respond generously to God's indescribable gift of grace. Freely receive, freely give.

The Rev. Melvin Amerson
The Methodist Foundation, Austin, Texas

Generosity as the Fruit of the Spirit   S 12

During my years as pastor I took a great interest in matters of Christian financial stewardship. I always believed God's people were created to be generous. The story of the offering being collected for the saints in Jerusalem (2 Cor. 8–9) is pivotal. In the midst of extreme poverty and persecution, the Macedonians were an example of generosity and joy. On the other hand, while rich with resources, the Corinthian church was not described as generous or joyful. I don't want to oversimplify the Corinthians' "easy" life, but as Paul writes, it is striking that to one he attributes joy and to another he does not. What does that mean for us?

Might it be there is a real connection between Holy Spirit joy and Holy Spirit generosity? If so, then we can see that giving really is "between me and God," in the sense that when our relationship with God is healthy and we are full of love for God, then our giving will be a joyous reflection. Our giving will be at a level that reflects gratitude that comes from the heart. Thus, it really is a spiritual matter.

My nephew, Larry, served as pastor of a church and a recently converted family was in worship when he preached on the tithe. The husband came through the line at the close of worship, thanked him for this message, and said, "Pastor, we're not only going to tithe, but we are going to give a hell of a lot more." You can't fault him for his gratitude!

Rev. David A. Rash
Stewardship Matters, Virginia

Generous Living   S 13

They rise in the darkness as a light for the upright;
they are gracious, merciful, and righteous.
It is well with those who deal generously and lend,
who conduct their affairs with justice.
For the righteous will never be moved;
they will be remembered forever. (Ps. 112:4–6)

This portion of Psalm 112 speaks to living generously. It defines such generous living as being gracious, merciful, and righteous. To live generously is to conduct our lives with justice. Generous living is much more than what we do with our money. We are called to be kind to one another and to all living things. We are called to deal with each other honestly, to be humble.

Robert Kennedy often quoted the Greek call, "To tame the savageness of man and make gentle the life of the world." That is a call to action, but also a call to living life generously. As followers of Jesus, we are called to live a generous life. He showed us the way to live generously: by welcoming the outcast, by overturning the tables of the money changers in the temple, by dining with the poor and healing the sick, by teaching, by forgiving, and by ultimately giving his life so that all might have life abundant.

I believe each of us is called to live wildly generous lives and that such generous living can transform us, our families, and our faith communities.

Mr. Rick Felton
The Episcopal Network for Stewardship

Give Us This Day S 14

"Give us this day our daily bread, and forgive us our sins, as we forgive those who sin against us."—The Lord's Prayer, Book of Common Prayer

It is the most universally recognized Christian prayer—its words formed on the lips of followers for two millennia. Week in and week out, we say it together in our churches; day in and day out, we say it in the silence of our hearts. Yet, as familiar as the Lord's Prayer is, it is all too easy to miss the power of its words to transform our hearts.

Think about it. After acknowledging the greatness of God and our desire to see God's will become reality here in our world, we come to the crux of the prayer: "O God, give us what we need to make it through today." Like the ancient Israelites in the wilderness who awoke each morning to find manna enough to get them through that particular day, so are we reminded of the importance of trusting daily in God, daring to be generous ourselves because we know that God will continue to provide.

The real power in the prayer is what follows: a plea that God would both forgive us and empower us to be generous enough to let go of the resentments that crowd and clutter our hearts. With our cup emptied of spiritual poison, it can be filled to overflowing with the gratitude for life and the joyful expectation that God alone can bring.

Our prayer in these circumstances: "Be generous this day to us, O God, even as we show a generosity of spirit to all those around us."

The Rev. C. K. Robertson, PhD
Canon to the Presiding Bishop for Ministry Beyond the
Episcopal Church

Gratitude—Children   S 15

Would we ever hesitate to tell our children about the love of God, to assure a grieving member of our hope in Christ, to pronounce pardon for the penitent, or healing for the sick? Would we ever withhold the sacrament from those who lift their hands to receive it? I pray not. Why then do we hesitate to preach stewardship, to teach it to each other, to form a steward's heart in our children? It is as much a part of faithful living as those other practices. In fact, it may be more than that, for how can we recognize God's love, pardon, and grace without gratitude? When we don't teach stewardship, we fail to build the foundation for all the rest of the Christian life. Without gratitude, we are blind to all God's blessings.

The Very Rev. Stephen Carlsen
Dean and Rector, Christ Church Cathedral,
Indianapolis, Indiana

Invest!   S 16

Many people have problems with giving money, yet most of them enjoy investing. Investing offers a promise of return; we experience excitement at the possibility our money will grow. We invest in the things that are important to us: our marriage, other meaningful relationships, our children's educations, national and personal security, our homes and neighborhoods. Some of us invest in the arts, or in cancer research, or in animal protection because these things are dear to us. When the church asks us to give, we are really being asked to invest, to invest in ministries and programs that change people's lives. Often these are programs that have changed or enhanced our own lives: meaningful worship, education, mission in places close by and far off. Our investment enables us to reduce the suffering of the poor and marginalized, open new options for the downtrodden, and offer new hope for those who feel lost. It is hard not to feel good about such investments. Who could resist?

The Rt. Rev. Robert W. Ihloff
Bishop of Maryland, Retired

Investing God's Gifts   S 17

In the parable of the talents, Jesus taught that we are to invest and not hoard what we have been entrusted with in building up God's kingdom. If we use what God has invested in us, God will multiply it into life-transforming blessings. As stewards, God wants us to invest our talents and financial resources for God's disciple-making enterprise. Let us give faithfully to honor the Lord for the many blessings showered upon us.

The Rev. Melvin Amerson
The Methodist Foundation, Austin, Texas

"It Is the Lord!"   S 18

The disciples recognized Jesus in the abundance of fish that were caught following his directive to cast their net on the other side of the boat. They seem to have known that it could only be the Lord who would lead them to such a generous haul, such an unprecedented amount of fish that their nets were not designed to handle, and yet they did not break. Jesus knew just where to canvas.

As the story continues, the disciples are asked to bring some of their catch to a waiting charcoal fire. This prepared barbecue already contained some fish as well as bread. The disciples' own contribution of fish combined with Jesus's bounty produced what must have been the best breakfast of their lives. And, again, it was in this shared meal and plenteous spread that they recognized Jesus. The comingled work of Jesus and the disciples yielded both miracle and revelation.

At its heart, stewardship is the recognition of God's generosity and our willingness to follow his example. It is a conscious decision to accept the life of abundance to which we are called, and to share this abundance with all of God's creation. How do we recognize the abundance that is right in front of us? Can we accept these gifts as truly received from the hand of God? And how do we work with Jesus to both make miracles and cultivate generosity? For it is in this generosity that Jesus is truly known.

The Rev. Suzanne M. Culhane
Canon for Stewardship, Diocese of Long Island

The Kingdom   S 19

As Paul writes in 1 Corinthians 12:12–31, the mystical body of Jesus Christ is a unity of interdependent members. We depend on the presence of every member of our community. And we depend on the diversity of gifts that each member brings to reflect God's kingdom. Only when all of our unique gifts are offered do we journey forward together in transformational ministries.

Through your support and through the abundant leadership of our many members, we connect people within our church, within our neighborhood—and indeed around the globe—more deeply to each other and more deeply to God.

We read to "strive for the greater gifts. And I will show you still a more excellent way" (1 Cor. 12:31). Our ministries in the church serve only a narrow path through God's kingdom if they are not wholly supported by each member. As you consider your commitments of work, wealth, and wisdom, do strive for the greater gifts, so that the many neighbors and members of our church will walk a more excellent way together—connected in the kingdom.

Julie Simonton
Officer for Congregational Development and Stewardship,
The Episcopal Diocese of Virginia

Love. Care. Give.   S 20

These are the three words that comprise a church's stewardship campaigns to raise pledges—pledges that fund God's mission. The three words betray their goal. It is a spiritual goal. We are being called to look at our lives. We are not being called to fill out a pledge card. We hope and believe that will happen during a stewardship campaign, but the issue is much more pressing.

The pledge card is to the stewardship campaign as the win registration card is to a marathon: a bit of paperwork at the end of a great struggle. When a person wins the Boston Marathon, there is a little paperwork to do after some Gatorade and perhaps a towel. That is what the pledge card is. The paperwork at the END of the race.

They say that prayer does not change God's mind; it changes ours. Real giving is about that which transforms us as givers from a place of gratitude—a place of seeing what we have in the context of our planet of people, most of whom have no plan for tomorrow's bread. Hence, the Lord's Prayer. . . . If you make $65,000, then you are sort of average in our church. And if you make that much money, then you are in the top 1 percent of the wealth of the world's population. Me too. We are rich. You can argue with me, but facts are facts.

That knowledge can do one of two things. It will either entrench me into a dark place of anger and shame and I will scrooge my way into isolation and clutch my wealth. Or, with the help of the Holy Spirit, I will see—really see—what I have as a gift from our Creator and not my precious salary or inheritance or entitlement.

We pledge to fund the church, which is the body of our Savior, Jesus the Christ. It is so simple to give. What is hard is the race before giving—the race, the struggle, the fight that is gratitude-seeing and that leads to the gift the way any fight leads to any victory.

The Rev. Canon Charles LaFond
Canon Steward, Saint John's Cathedral, Denver, Colorado

More Than a Supporting Character   S 21

> There was a Levite, a native of Cyprus, Joseph, to whom the apostles gave the name Barnabas (which means "son of encouragement"). He sold a field that belonged to him, then brought the money, and laid it at the apostles' feet. (Acts 4:36–37)

He first appears as little more than a footnote in the story of the early Church, but Barnabas was far more than just a supporting character. We learn that his real name was Joseph, a Jew from the priestly tribe of Levi. We also learn that he was not from Jerusalem, or anywhere in Palestine. Rather, he hailed from the island country of Cyprus in the Mediterranean. All he had to do was open his mouth, and you knew from his dialect that he was an outsider.

Barnabas's tale does not end with money, but begins there. More to the point, it begins with vision. His stewardship was not simply a matter of "paying his dues." No, his giving was a tangible statement of faith in response to what he saw happening in the apostolic community. He experienced the Spirit there and responded with generosity.

And he went one step further. When the apostles refused to welcome a more questionable newcomer, Saul of Tarsus, that former persecutor-turned-convert, along came Barnabas. He who was generous with his money was generous also with his friendship, first vouching for the unwelcome Saul, and then eventually taking him on as an apprentice in ministry. No wonder he became known as "the Encourager."

May we dare to be like Barnabas, and live not as supporting characters, but as generous supporters with our treasure and our friendship.

The Rev. C. K. Robertson, PhD
Canon to the Presiding Bishop for Ministry Beyond the
Episcopal Church

Palm Sunday C and Christ the King C, Proper 29C   S 22

Luke 23:42 "Jesus, remember me when you come into your kingdom."

Jesus speaks about money and wealth throughout the Gospels. In fact, the only subject Jesus speaks about more than money is the kingdom of God. And in doing so, Jesus is not only telling us amazing stories, describing what the kingdom of God is like, he is teaching us how to be good and righteous citizens in this kingdom. He is teaching us—as we hear in the collect from the Book of Common Prayer on page 236—how "the peoples of the earth, divided and enslaved by sin, may be freed and brought together under his gracious rule."

When Jesus speaks about the kingdom of God more than anything else, he is also teaching us to speak about the kingdom of God more than anything else. When Jesus speaks about money more than anything else—except the kingdom of God—he is teaching us to robustly speak about and engage our connection to wealth. These are our calls. These are at the core of our identity: turning to the Cross, experiencing God's love, and then *telling* others about it. And then turning to the generous gifts God has given us, experiencing God's love, and *proclaiming to* others about it. We walk in Jesus's love through God's kingdom by proclaiming through word and example the generous Good News of God in Christ.

Julie Simonton
Officer for Congregational Development and Stewardship,
The Episcopal Diocese of Virginia

Penang Curry   S 23

I wonder if the future of the stewardship of money in the church (pledging) is not mostly about simplicity rather than generosity. I mean, how can we give if we are spending at absolute capacity to keep up with the Joneses?

As stewardship season gathers steam in churches with a parade of letters, sermons, and announcements about giving and pledging to the mission of the church, it is clear to me that the problem for most of us is not that we are ungenerous to the church, but that we are simply so financially tapped out that giving is hard without very careful budgeting.

The ability to give money away is not so much about what we give as it is about what we spend. What if we stopped talking about giving and started talking about what it means to follow a Savior whose possessions amounted to some cloth, some leather, and a walking stick?

When I make penang curry, I am aware I am eating something beautiful. Thai restaurants around town charge $15 for a bowl of this stuff. And they should! It is delicious. But the other day I did the math, and it turns out that if I make a big batch of curry and freeze what I do not eat that night, I can make a meal that, though stunning in its beauty, taste, and nutrition, costs me less than a dollar a serving. I just took the ingredients and divided their cost up by the bowl: a spoonful of red curry paste, two Thai eggplants, eight sweet basil leaves, one quarter of a carrot, four spears of canned baby corn, a strip of bell pepper, a cauliflower floret, four green beans, an eighth of an onion, a quarter of a can of coconut milk, some broth or water, a teaspoon full of peanut butter, and a dash of fish sauce. Voila! Dinner for a buck.

"Live simply so that others may simply live" is one of my favorite aphorisms. There is nothing particularly Christian about it, and yet the saying would make Jesus's knees go weak with joy. I wonder if the key to being generous people is less about being rich and more about living such simple, good lives—grateful that we can see the beauty in things like a bowl of Thai curry: the heat on our hands from the clay, the steam on our face from the bowl, the tastes of the curry on our tongue, the crunch of the vegetables. What keeps us from giving is often not greed but rather carelessness. Perhaps what is needed is not money but mindfulness.

The Rev. Canon Charles LaFond
Canon Steward, Saint John's Cathedral, Denver, Colorado

Possessions   S 24

Over the past three years I have been blessed to observe Maundy Thursday with our mission to the homeless. I am inspired each time by many of these fine people, and even more by their view on a life that looks anything but joyful to me when I hear them tell it. But when the invitation to name the thanksgivings and blessings of our lives comes during the Prayers of the People, they go on and on. These people that seemingly have nothing cannot seem to stop finding reasons to be thankful. I have found the same reality in my visits to prisons and jails. This is startling to me because often in our churches, when the same invitation is offered, I hear, instead, dead silence. And I always wonder, who is really in prison? Who is really homeless?

We live in a consumeristic society. In fact, our economy is basically based on our consuming the things we desire more than need, and also those things consuming us. A spiritual exercise for a Christian living in this society has to be asking questions about not only what we consume, but how our possessions and desires consume us. The wisdom of Jesus, throughout the gospel, is that we must consume to live, but we can never be fully alive if we don't give in equal measure. This Western world we live in is based on the concept that we will be happy once we possess all that we desire. The wisdom of the gospel is exactly the opposite. The wisdom of Jesus is this: it is not what we take up, but what we give up, that makes us rich.

The Rt. Rev. Gregory H. Rickel
Bishop, Diocese of Olympia

Preaching by Our Deeds   S 25

Francis of Assisi is often quoted as having said, "Preach the gospel in all things; use words when necessary." It is a powerful statement. Unfortunately, it is not a quote, but a restating of what he wrote in *The Earlier Rule* (1221), chapter 17, "Preachers": "Let all the brothers (and sisters), however, preach by their deeds. . . ."

In chapter 17 of *The Earlier Rule*, Francis states that one must conform to the rules of the church, but he goes further to note that preaching is about what one does. He speaks of an "interior spirit" that seeks to live out the gospel and is both proclamation and good works.

The vast majority of stewardship that I have encountered focuses on three things: the necessity of treasure, exhortation to tithe, and, in no small amount, a lot of "shoulds." When I served in Atlanta, it took time for me to fully understand the words the bishop, the Rt. Rev. Frank K. Allan, said: "The church does not need your money. It will survive and not even the gates of hell shall prevail against it. You need to give for the salvation of your soul." These words have drawn me to Francis and his belief that we give for our salvation, but we are to see in our deeds that there must be a full manifestation of living the gospel.

Preaching by our deeds is to hold up what Jesus demands of us and what it means to live the gospel life. This is not a seasonal matter, but continually teaching through our deeds to reflect the generosity of the gospel life. Let our deeds, those of faithful and loving commitments, be the mark of our stewardship. We need to move from the call for treasure to do this or that—or even the call for how much to give—to a call for generous, loving, and just deeds for God's people. Let us preach by our deeds.

The Rt. Rev. John L. Rabb
Bishop Suffragan (retired), Episcopal Diocese of Maryland

Presence   S 26

How weighty to me are your thoughts, O God!
How vast is the sum of them!

I try to count them—they are more than the sand;
I come to the end—I am still with you. (Ps. 139:17–18)

As we consider stewardship, we often find ourselves taking an inventory of what we have, our physical possessions. This kind of asset accounting isn't a bad thing for us to do as we consider what we will give to God's service, but maybe stewardship should begin with thoughts about spiritual being rather than physical property. Maybe stewardship of our souls and what we take in is as important as our possessions and what we can give out.

The other day I was talking with a colleague over lunch about Eastern religion and the idea of mindfulness. He said, "As much as I feel breathing techniques and the focus on being in the moment, mindfulness, are of value, mindfulness can be a little vague and unfocused for me. I think meditation should have a focus beyond myself and my surroundings. I think we should use disciplines like St. Ignatius' *Spiritual Exercises* to develop courage and resolve to truly be in the present moment."

I remember my mother's daily discipline of devotional books, Bible reading, and prayer—the stewardship of her soul. If I ever doubted that God cared for me, my mother's prayer and love were enough to help dispel that doubt. If we are honest with ourselves, we must confess that there are moments when God appears to be distant or absent. Psalm 139 calls the disciplined soul to remember that even when we have tried to hide, God is still with us.

The Rev. Fred Weimert
Vice President of the Board, Central Maryland Ecumenical
Council

Responding to God's Blessing S 27

The apostle Paul said, "On the first day of every week each of you is to put aside and save whatever extra you earn, so that collections need not be taken when I come" (1 Cor. 16:2). In this verse he informs believers that their offering is more than an occasional gift; it is worship. Today, we also present our regular offering as a part of worshipping God. As

God has blessed, you, may you respond to God's blessing in your worship through giving.

The Rev. Melvin Amerson
The Methodist Foundation, Austin, Texas

Scarcity   S 28

I'm reminded of Andrew, a member of the first church I ever served. He was by no means a wealthy man, but was obsessed by what little he did have. Andrew could never enjoy anything; he was continually distracted, prepossessed by consuming concern about what lawyers would call his worldly estate. The sheer weight of daily life, paying the bills, household maintenance, deciding when to trade in or to trade up, storm windows or screens, the furnace, the phone, the front porch—these details so dominated his existence that he knew not one moment's peace, one fragment of true relaxation. Andrew lived in hell, and his hell was not the *absence* of worldly goods, but their presence, their never-ending, ever-demanding presence.

> The world is too much with us; late and soon,
> Getting and spending, we lay waste our powers:

wrote Wordsworth of his times, 150 years ago. Think of it this way. If you dedicate your entire life to the accumulation of stuff—property, possessions, prizes—then slowly but surely that stuff piles up, builds higher and higher walls. Protective walls, some claim, but protective from what? Might it not become almost impossible, in time, to reach over those towering walls and make contact with another human being? Recently on NPR I heard cosmologist Brian Swimme decry how self-storage facilities are able to receive purchases we make directly. We don't have to receive what we purchase at our homes or offices first. They can be shipped directly from the retailer to the storage unit!

The Rev. Dr. J. Barrie Shepherd
Minister Emeritus of historic First Presbyterian Church,
New York, New York

Small and Mighty Churches—
Average Weekly Impact   S 29

I don't believe Jesus ever said, "Go forth and build up your ASA"—that's "Average Sunday Attendance," a frequently cited church statistic. I don't recall any mention of counting heads, or building up of endowments, or having the fanciest church buildings. Jesus did say a lot about taking up our share of his mission by loving our neighbors, promoting justice, feeding the hungry, and caring for the widows and orphans; we are called to care for the people who have been pushed to the margins or forgotten. He spoke of preaching Good News to the poor and setting captives free. In his ministry he taught us, by word and example, that mercy and service are the highest priorities in the kingdom of heaven. We are to do as he has done.

Many good Christian people fall captive to the worldly standard that more is better: the ASA or the financial balance sheet or the historic beauty of our buildings is more important than the number of lives touched by that congregation's ministry. In the Diocese of Maryland, we now give greater priority to the AWI (Average Weekly Impact) rather than the ASA (Average Sunday Attendance). It's not that attendance doesn't matter; it does. But the number of lives each congregation touches in a given week matters far more.

I know of many congregations that are small and poor, yet mighty and fruitful in witnessing to the gospel through their actions as well as their words. Those congregations have an AWI that is many times higher than their ASA. The congregation's ministry touches many lives—far more than the church attendance records or the balance sheet. In what ways does your church bring gospel impact to the lives of people outside your doors? We have a treasure—the gospel—to share; do we hoard this treasure or do we spend and spread it to people in need?

The Rt. Rev. Chilton R. Knudsen
Assistant Bishop of Maryland

Stewards of God's Message   S 30

> Do not neglect to do good and to share what you have, for such
> sacrifices are pleasing to God. (Heb. 13:16)

The practice of stewardship goes beyond the idea of charitable church giving and incorporates a desire to care and protect the gifts that God has given us. In practicing stewardship, we must be mindful to remember that all things come from and belong to God. There is plenty for all to have shelter and to eat and to grow and flourish. This invites us to ponder the way in which we are to use creation. This notion is at the very heart of stewardship.

It is easy to slip into a gospel of prosperity, if wealth and blessings are the focus. We should not seek to give so that in return, we might have wealth and blessings. The gospel of grace invites us to consider a response to how God has acted in creating and redeeming. With the gift of forgiveness, eternal life, and all of creation, what shall we do? We get to ask ourselves how we might act as a steward of God's message and God's kingdom as we journey through life.

The Rt. Rev. C. Andrew Doyle
Ninth Bishop of Texas

Stewards of Love   S 31

> Owe no one anything, except to love one another;
> for the one who loves another has fulfilled the law. (Rom. 13:8)

In the fall we celebrate Thanksgiving. It is a day when we give thanks for what God has done for us, and on that day we measure what God has done in physical ways. So it is not surprising that the liturgy for Thanksgiving Day normally includes some reading from Deuteronomy. We may read from Deuteronomy 8 about God giving us wealth and power, or we may read from litany in Deuteronomy 26 about our bringing first fruits of the harvest to God. All of these thoughts are appropriate for that day of thanksgiving and for thoughts on our stewardship as returning from God's physical gifts.

But as Christians, our understandings of God's greatest gift is not centered in wealth, power, or abundant harvests. Instead God's greatest gift is the love of God that is embodied in Jesus, our Christ. Paul tells us in Romans 13:8–10 that this love of God calls us to be stewards of love. In the Gospel summations of the greatest commandments, we are told that there are only two: to love God and to love our neighbor as ourself. The first letter of John pushes those commandments to be stewards of God's love even further when he says, "We love because he first loved us. Those who say, "I love God," and hate their brothers or sisters, are liars; for those who do not love a brother or sister whom they have seen, cannot love God whom they have not seen." (1 John 4:19–20)

The Rev. Fred Weimert
Vice President of the Board, Central Maryland Ecumenical
Council

Time Is a Creature of God S 32

Time is a creature of God with which humanity wrestles. There never seems to be enough time and it always goes by too quickly. As the creator of time, God invites us to see time as a gift; an opportunity to share ourselves with others. Humanity is not meant to serve time, but time is meant to serve humanity and God's desire for reconciled relationships among the brothers and sisters of his own making.

Every person is given the same number of hours in a day, week, month, and year. There is a time for everything; to work, to sow, and to lose. (Eccles. 3:1–13) How we use this time is up to us. We manage our time to avoid being possessed by time, work, and disruptions of a living that serves other gods. As Christian stewards, we are invited to commit our time to God and to share ourselves with others.

The Rt. Rev. C. Andrew Doyle
Ninth Bishop of Texas

The Tithe   S 33

> Jacob said to God, "of all that you give me I will surely give one-tenth to you." (Gen. 28:22)

After an astounding dream, Jacob made this promise to God. In gratitude, he promised gratitude. That is exactly what the tithe is meant to teach us. God has given us everything, and we return a bit of it. We Christians make our tithe to the church. The church is the place, above all others, that exists to proclaim the Good News of Jesus Christ and share God's love with the world. Our thank offering sustains work that transforms lives.

It's tempting for us to consider the tithe and to rationalize it away. Ten percent is a lot, and that's scary. Never mind that we get to keep ninety percent. I've heard lots of ways we love to convince ourselves that we don't really need to tithe. But here's the thing. The tithe is actually a pretty good amount. For nearly all of us, that kind of giving makes us aware of our gift. It is more than a token, thought-free gift. Most of us will probably have to make some choices to spend less here or there because of our giving.

What a gift that is! When we stop taking our "stuff" for granted, we can begin to be grateful for all that we have. When we stop taking our giving for granted, we can savor the joy that comes from supporting life-changing, world-changing work and worship.

The Rev. Canon Scott Gunn
Executive Director, Forward Movement, Cincinnati, Ohio

Treasure   S 34

Must we give away all we have, like the rich young ruler in the Gospels? Realistically we are not about to do that, whether out of greed, fear, or wise precaution—of this I do not dare to judge. I know my own mixed motivations too well. However, it may not be too late to begin a weaning process; to begin to live more simply, so that others may simply live; to learn that there are two ways to be rich: to have plenty of money, or fewer needs. Long before the age of psychiatry, Jesus showed amazing insight into the desires that motivate us. And on this subject of money he hit the nail on the head: where your treasure is, there will your heart be also. In other words, if you want to know what you value most, that for which you live, look for that around which you build your days.

The story is told of a missionary family in China who were placed, during the revolution, under house arrest. One day soldiers arrived to tell them, to their great relief, that they were soon to be allowed to return to the USA, but they could only take 200 pounds of belongings. They dug out some scales and the deliberations began. One had favorite books, another a collection of Chinese porcelain. One insisted on his new typewriter; someone else favorite toys. Finally, after much bargaining, they managed to whittle their goods down to 200 pounds. The soldiers returned.

"Are you ready?"

"Yes."

"Did you weigh everything?"

"Yes."

"Did you weigh the children?" And there it all went: books, clothing, typewriter, porcelain, toys. All of it turned into trash. Suddenly this family knew where their treasure was; where their hearts belonged.

The Rev. Dr. J. Barrie Shepherd
Minister Emeritus of historic First Presbyterian Church,
New York, New York

A Vow of Poverty?   S 35

Prior to doing a presentation of the four pillars of the Franciscan tradition (poverty, minority, fraternity, and itinerancy), I was asked by someone why I would speak on poverty. He said, "I have been in poverty, and there is no good news there!" The Franciscan understanding of poverty is about learning to live dependently on the grace of God. It is not to literally be without, but to see that all is from God; all is gift.

When we think of what we have as our possession, we can become greedy and fearful. When we see all we have as gift, we are more inclined to be thankful and generous. This is what stewardship is all about.

When we see all we have as gift, we avoid the two great sins that the Franciscan tradition addresses: self-sufficiency and exalting destitution. The first is when we think all we have is ours: we earned it, or we are entitled to it. Such thinking results in the proverbial "there is not enough." If I think I do not have enough, I will not share or be generous. Such thinking dominates much of our culture.

Exalting destitution is equally as sinful. It is shameful for any society when people do not have what they need for the necessities of life: food, shelter, employment, education, and health care. Francis's understanding of poverty was never to exalt not having what you need. Francis called on us to be generous so that all may have what they need.

For Francis, material poverty distinguishes between need and want. Need is what is required to have a fulfilling, loving, and faithful life. What we want often comes out of fear, of hoarding, of self-sufficiency.

It may seem strange to speak of poverty when addressing mostly middle-class church people. I am persuaded that if we can move from possession to gift and from want to need, we, with thankfulness, can be better stewards of all we have—since all we have is from God.

The Rt. Rev. John L. Rabb
Bishop Suffragan (retired), Episcopal Diocese of Maryland

The Way We Scream   S 36

Perhaps we are not greedy people. Perhaps we are simply frightened people and our withholding of money is simply the way we have chosen to scream.

It is hard to tell why I was not born in Somalia or an Eskimo village or the Bronx. I do not understand the way God makes choices and do not for a moment believe that the inequalities in the planet among humans is anything other than the result of human greed systems. But for some reason, I am privileged to have been born into a free society and into a place and time with the resources to provide me with food, housing, and even money for some of life's luxuries.

I understand that the symbol of my gratitude is my investment into God's mission through the church, which I believe has the capacity to do good in the world. I believe our church deserves the money. I do not believe that of every church or diocese, but I believe that of mine because I see the fruit.

My work as a priest, like that of every priest and every baptized Christian, is to see the drop of cool water on a flower petal as we pass by, and be amazed by what God has done for humanity and all of life on this planet in this cosmos. First, of course, I must be able to stop and see these details. I must have a rule of life that slows me down and roots me to the daily experience of the glory of God through this planet's life.

We do not raise funds for the church with big crosses, candles, stewardship campaigns, and pledge cards. We raise money for the mission of God, in this time, by reminding each other of all of which we might be grateful and with which we have been charged as stewards. When that happens, we have trouble keeping track of the money we raise.

The Rev. Canon Charles LaFond
Canon Steward, Saint John's Cathedral, Denver, Colorado

Section V

Giving Meditations

All Is Gift   G 1

"All things come of thee, O God, and of thine own have we given thee."

—The Offertory, Book of Common Prayer

Each time we come together for the Eucharist, we hear scripture read and explicated, we profess our faith and confess our sins, we pray and praise God, and we share a word of peace with friends and newcomers alike. All this before we approach the Table and share in Holy Communion. And we do one thing more: we open our wallets or checkbooks . . . and we give. This is no small thing. Is it simply a practical matter—support for the work of the church? Though certainly practical, it is more. It is a statement of faith.

How seductively easy it is in this world of ours to fall prey to the age-old trap of supposing that we are self-sufficient, that we are in charge, in control, and entitled to the treasures we possess, even as we are fearful of losing them. The result is either smugness on the one hand or constant worry on the other. It takes only one moment, one reversal of fortune in any manner of forms, to hit us with the hard reality that we are not in control; we are not in charge. The good news is that we need not wait to acknowledge our dependence on God. Each time we open our hands to give, we let go of some of that self-sufficiency and entitlement, acknowledging once more that all that we have and all that we are is truly gift, no matter how it comes to us.

The Rev. C. K. Robertson, PhD
Canon to the Presiding Bishop for Ministry Beyond the
Episcopal Church

Compassion for the Poor   G 2

What about the person with the sign that asks for help? Are they really down and out? Is their job to look for a daily take? Will they spend it on drink? Do they merit my charitable dollar?

Driving can become an occasion for moral judgment or for shutting off feelings. The presence of obvious poverty can stir us. We would like to know that a gesture of generosity might make some difference, even for thirty minutes, and salve our own consciences. Our gift is no solution to an obvious train wreck of a life, only a modest Band-Aid.

Consider Pope Francis's outreach to the poor. He well knows he is not altering difficult circumstances, but his purpose remains steady. What makes your life different from the needy person's? Francis suggests the major reason is luck. You were born into a place where you could prosper; the other was not. Perhaps bad choices were made, but the key acknowledgement on your part is that you do not "deserve" your circumstances any more than the penitent "deserved" theirs. Francis suggests that if you give, the most important thing is to acknowledge the other person's humanity. They too are a child of God. Look them in the eye as you give. Touch their hand as you give. Say something that wishes them well. The perceptible change will be in your own heart, not theirs. Your dollar acknowledges that you have a fullness in your own life, more than you deserve. Live the fullness well and honorably. Your response to your gift is to say "thank you"—not to them, but for what you have been given. May our compassion for an unfortunate reveal our sincere gratitude for what we have not merited and faithful stewardship of our gifts.

Dr. Mary Blair
Chair, Stewardship Team, Cathedral of the Incarnation,
Baltimore, Maryland

Firstness G 3

There is something I learned early on in the stewardship training I had. It was the idea of "firstness." Yes, "firstness." I'm not sure that is really a word, but it works. The idea of "firstness" is making your gift to the church first. If you write checks monthly for your bills, make the one to the church the first one you write; when you budget, make your gift the first thing you set aside. So often our gifts to God and the church are an afterthought, given only if something is left over. The practice of "firstness" guards against this. It reminds us that this is how God gives to us, first, out of abundance, fully. If we truly believe that everything we have God gave to us, then the 10 percent we give back—first—is our practice of acknowledging that reality. That gift back is the first thing, not the last thing, not the "if I have something left." No matter how much you give, maybe even more important than the amount, is **when** you give it, and the priority in which you give. Start with this practice: whatever you can give, give it first.

The Rt. Rev. Gregory H. Rickel
Bishop, Diocese of Olympia

Generous Example G 4

Our annual mission trip to Tijuana, Mexico, was a wondrous week of hard work for our brave band of bodacious builders. Under the hot sun with nothing but hand tools, we constructed a small home for a poor family in one the poorest neighborhoods of this border city. La Señora, whose family would live in the house once we were done, joined us every day. The two English words she knew well, and used often, were "Thank you." She watched as the footings were dug and the cement poured. She watched the walls being framed and the roof laid out. She watched the stucco being applied. She watched as our young workers slipped away in groups of two or three to visit the small *tienda* in the neighborhood for a refreshing diet soda.

On the last day of our labors, La Señora was nowhere to be seen. At midmorning, she came walking up the dusty hillside with heavy plastic bags in each hand—each bag held three-liter-size bottles of diet soda that she handed to our young workers with a quiet "Thank you." We were left speechless by her generosity. She could not afford the gift, but she had been watching. She saw our needs. She witnessed the source of our refreshment. And she gave us what we had been really thirsting for all week long—profound evidence of Christian generosity. We were deeply satisfied, and in tears. May we all follow her generous example.

Mr. Jerry Campbell
Capital Campaign Consultant, Episcopal Church
Foundation

George's Gift G 5

Through the sanctuary doors I saw a man sitting alone. From his suspendered overalls I knew it was George, one of our flock whom I normally visited in his 1900s vintage bungalow. We have often sat on his porch swing—an old car seat—and talked of his Mary, long dead, and his two adult sons, both mentally handicapped from birth. "George, may I sit with you?" I had asked.

"Of course, Rev. Jane," he whispered. "Just not there. The Lord is there. He comes and we talk about things."

I saw a large brown paper bag on the Communion Table and inquired if it was George's. "It's for the Lord's needs, just for him," he replied. The bag was filled with $400 of pennies—a copper treasure earned from his collection of empty bottles along Route 46 that ran through our old mining town all the way to New York City. My Scotish frugality flared up. The money could pay George's electric bill and buy food for months. But that was poor and narrow thinking. The angel's vision revealed to George the Lord's need for beauty—something pretty—like fixing that colored glass window. And so his pennies became rainbows of light streaming onto worshippers whose lives saw little beauty.

Such lavish unselfishness echoes the woman at Bethany who broke an alabaster jar, extravagantly pouring out its expensive oils to anoint Jesus's weary body. Sheer waste—it could have been used for the poor, the scornful warned. But Jesus said, "Let her alone . . . she has performed a good service for me" (Mark 14:6).

So be it.

The Rev. Jane R. Bearden, STM, Hon.rt.
The Presbytery of Baltimore, Maryland

Gift of Shoes   G 6

One Sunday, just as a parishioner and I were leaving our small mission church, Joseph appeared at the door. We invited him in, and he shared his story. Almost two years before, he had fled terrorism in northern Nigeria. He made a harrowing six-month journey to the United States through South and Central America. Upon crossing the border into San Diego, he was detained for one year, then relocated to a men's shelter thirty miles north of San Diego—and two miles from our church. We were the only church within walking distance.

The next week, from quietly generous parishioners, shoes appeared for Joseph along with an umbrella and a jacket to weather the rainy season. Joseph came early on Sundays to sweep the sidewalks, join the greeters, sing in the choir, and worship with us. He helped our small church to grow.

Then one Thursday in Easter, another man came to the church door. Jason was barefoot. He was a construction worker who had fallen on hard times. The night before in a nearby park, his shoes were stolen.

"This is embarrassing," Jason said, "but could you could help me get a pair of shoes? Anything size ten will do." Joseph happened to be at the church, and by this time had acquired two pairs of shoes. Sensing Jason's need, Joseph asked if he could offer his shoes.

I answered, "Yes. What size are they?"

"Size ten." Joseph took off and handed over his shoes and socks. Jason put them on. His relief was palpable. Now both men, who continue to reside at the men's shelter, are part of our church. They found us. It was our challenge and blessing to meet them where they were, just as God meets us all, and let God do the rest.

The Rev. Dr. Laura Sheridan-Campbell
Vicar, Holy Cross Church, Carlsbad, California

Giving and Receiving Dignity   G 7

While I served as bishop in the Diocese of Maine, we pursued a productive companion diocese relationship with the Diocese of Haiti. My first visit to Haiti was shocking; I saw the ravages of poverty as I had never seen before. Starving children with swollen bellies and stick-thin limbs were everywhere. I felt deep guilt about the disparity between my privileged life and the bare subsistence I saw.

I toured many Diocese of Haiti schools, clinics, programs, and agencies. Each place I visited, I was received with songs, speeches, and genuine hospitality. Everywhere I visited a gift was presented: a carving, a painting, a bracelet, a piece of metal sculpture, an embroidered shirt or scarf. This generosity and my unprocessed guilt prompted me to say to the kind Haitian priest who was my driver, "Can you please tell the people not to give me any more gifts? I wish they would take the money they have spent on gifts for me, and use it to buy food for their starving children. I already have too many things."

His looked at me with kind eyes as he said, "So, Bishop, you want me to tell the people not to give you gifts, but to save that money and buy food for their children? Oh, Bishop, don't take away our dignity! It is our great human dignity to GIVE. Just say, 'Thank you.'"

I have never forgotten that moment. Indeed, human dignity is expressed in our giving, and in our willingness to receive we affirm that dignity in others.

The Rt. Rev. Chilton R. Knudsen
Assistant Bishop of Maryland

Homeless Gift of Coffee   G 8

In my urban cathedral, we have a relationship with those experiencing homelessness in our community. It is a joy to accompany some of these persons as they rebuild their lives and find a permanent home. One such man, despite substantial mental illness, found the courage and accepted God's grace to overcome his challenges. One afternoon he approached me and asked me to go with him to Starbucks. He wanted to buy me a cup of coffee. I was hesitant, uncomfortable to be given such a gift by someone with so little. He told me, "This means more to me than you can know." I was humbled. Do we think of giving as an obligation or as a blessing, as a duty or as an occasion for thanks? Ever since that precious cup of coffee, I know that giving is its own blessing, and I try to cultivate a thankful heart like my friend at Starbucks that day.

The Very Rev. Stephen Carlsen
Dean and Rector, Christ Church Cathedral,
Indianapolis, Indiana

Joy-Filled Giving   G 9

When it comes to stewardship, one of the most well-known biblical citations is 2 Corinthians 9:7, "Each of you must give as you have made up your mind, not reluctantly or under compulsion, for God loves a *cheerful* giver." The Greek adjective used here is *hilaros,* commonly translated as "cheerful," but also defined as "joyful, not grudging." There is no record of the English word "hilarious" being used before the nineteenth century, but it is clearly derived from the earlier Greek usage, and has been defined variously as "cheerful, lively, merry, or boisterously joyful." In popular usage, *hilarious* refers to anything that is extremely funny, accompanied by over-the-top laughter.

Clearly, Paul, who wrote to the Corinthians urging them to give to those in need in Jerusalem, did not have in mind that they should be rolling on the floor doubled over with laughter during the collection. The need to help others in need was serious business, not a joke. But he *did* remind his readers that their giving should make them joy-filled. Givers should be at least as happy in their giving as those on the receiving end of their gifts.

Contrast Paul's teaching with the way the offering is regularly collected in many of our North American churches. Usually accompanied by stiff faces, still bodies, funeral-like music and highly regimented pageantry, the offering is often the most somber time in the service. But not so in many of our growing congregations, nor in much of the rest of the world—especially in Africa, Latin America, and the Caribbean. I will never forget the exuberant sense of celebration a group of us visiting from the United States witnessed a few years ago during the offering at the Anglican cathedral in Accra, Ghana. The music was lively and the worshipers were joyful as they left their seats holding their gifts of money in their hands, singing energetically as they danced to the offering baskets at the front of the church. The whole ritual lasted maybe a half hour—but who noticed the time? I and the other Episcopal leaders visiting that day felt as though we had experienced a bit of heaven, and, my, oh my, we *gave* at that offering.

How is the offering done—no, *celebrated*—in your church? Would it be possible, at least occasionally, to invite worshipers to leave their seats as they are able and personally take their offerings up to the altar? Would they be given permission to express joy in doing so, perhaps in singing or in moving their hands and feet? When I bid the offering at a parish during my episcopal visitations, I usually say the following words:

"And now, we come to the 'funnest' part of our Eucharistic celebration: we get to give. I want you to give until it puts a smile on your face; if you're not smiling, then you haven't given enough. So walk in love, as *Christ loves you and gave everything for you*, an offering and sacrifice to God. Amen."

The Rt. Rev. Eugene Taylor Sutton
Bishop, Episcopal Diocese of Maryland

A Lesson from Las Vegas   G 10

Philippians 1:9–11

I'm not a gambler, but there I was—out for a stroll along the Las Vegas Strip. It is lined with luxury casinos and resort hotels teeming with people taking chances on a quick fortune. I was on a break from a national conference on baptismal ministry. The afternoon sun was bearing down, and I needed a respite.

Drawn by the opulence of one particular hotel, I entered the ornate lobby and saw beyond it a bright atrium adorned with lavish plants and flowers. In the middle of it was a circular bar, with plush seats and nattily dressed servers. I ordered the House Special Cosmopolitan, served straight up and ice cold. It was a pricey treat—with tax and tip, about twenty bucks—but what refreshment! I thought, "How pleasant it would be to do something like this just once each week for an hour or so. My twenty bucks a week would hardly be missed."

Then it hit me: my twenty bucks a week would fund a thousand dollars a year over and above my annual pledge. It could help support a soup kitchen or a homeless shelter in ways that would offer countless folk a far more enduring form of refreshment than my twenty-dollar cocktail. So, I propose a toast: here's to God's great abundance, and to our wise stewardship of it.

The Rt Reverend Joe Goodwin Burnett
Tenth Bishop of Nebraska, 2003–2011

Suggested uses for the above meditation: The season after Epiphany; the season after Pentecost

More Than I Can Afford to Give   G 11

I looked at her pledge card and set it aside. At first, I thought it was a mistake. She couldn't possibly afford to give that much. I knew her well. She was among the first to greet me when I came to serve the parish, and was a regular volunteer in the church office. She was rarely absent on a Sunday morning. I knew that she lived off a minimal income and relied on assistance from a variety of community resources. I had visited her in her home often enough to know that she eschewed luxury, and obviously embraced a simple lifestyle out of necessity.

"Of course it's more than I can afford to give," she said. "But that's the point isn't it? I can't afford a lot of the things that other people do to make them happy, but I finally realized that if I'm very careful with my money, I can do something that makes me VERY happy indeed: give it away. You wouldn't want to deprive an old lady of her happiness would you?" And she gave me a smile that said I ought not to argue. So I finished my tea, tucked her pledge card back into my pocket, and left her happiness intact.

Mr. Jerry Campbell
Captial Campaign Consultant, Episcopal Church
Foundation

Ownership   G 12

Jesus is challenged by the issue of ownership (Luke 20:24–25). Caesar's face is on a coin. Is it Caesar's? Is it God's? Jesus never answers. He only says, "Render to Caesar what is Caesar's and to God what is God's." However, like any righteous Jew, Jesus knows all that is found is owned by God. "The earth is the Lord's and the fullness thereof." Of course, if you could find "anything" that did belong to Caesar and not to God, give it to him.

The Rev. Dr. William L. Bearden, Hon.rt.
The Presbytery of Baltimore, Maryland

Prayer, Fasting, and
Almsgiving during Lent   G 13

Like most Catholics and many other Christians, growing up I tended to approach the months leading up to Lent with a mild sense of dread. I looked forward to Easter, but not to Friday: fasting, prayer services, and giving some of my allowance. Later, with a wife and three children, we discovered a family Lenten formation program called "Operation Rice Bowl," run by an organization we were vaguely aware of called Catholic Relief Services (CRS).

Somewhat to my surprise, God had a Lenten plan for me. Thirteen years ago I joined the staff of CRS and became responsible for overseeing a bunch of programs, including "Operation Rice Bowl." I learned that Rice Bowl engages millions of U.S. Catholics and other people of goodwill in prayer, fasting, and almsgiving.

Leaning into this role, I came to understand that Lent was first and foremost a chance for Christians to take stock of our relationship with God and to seek Jesus in the face of each other. Instead of feeling mildly guilty during Lent, we can make more space in our hearts, minds, and bodies for the presence of Jesus's healing for our brokenness. And it was about converting our Lenten prayer and fasting into tangible gifts so we can help spread God's love to our "neighbors" locally and around the world who are struggling. Giving alms during Lent becomes a tangible expression of our prayer.

My organization deeply appreciates the $12 million raised each year from millions of Catholics and other people of goodwill during Lent, because it allows us to fund antihunger programs around the world and in the United States. But it is even more valuable when the giving is part of a deeper and more personal Lenten experience of prayer and fasting. Those elements move us from a simple act of charity to a moment of real solidarity with some 800 million of our brothers and sisters around the world who are praying to the same God but go to bed during Lent without enough food to eat.

Brian Joseph Backe
Senior Director for U.S. Programs and Resources for
Catholic Relief Services

Proportional Giving— Don't Settle for Less G 14

"Give until it hurts" is not a sound way to think of our giving. "Give until it feels good" is the secret to giving. When your gift brings you deep satisfaction, you are adequately supporting something in which you truly believe. The way to measure such a gift is by figuring out what proportion of your income it represents. If you don't do this, your giving will be governed more by the dollar amount. In the days I contributed on the basis of what I thought would a "respectable" gift, I was not a happy giver. I resented being asked; I detested everything about the process. I felt pressured to give more than I wanted to give. Then I was introduced to proportional giving. The first time I figured out what percentage of my income my giving represented, I was shocked. It was a lot less than I thought. I decided I wanted to give a larger percentage and my giving went up; so did my spirits. I felt good about my gift for the first time. It actually represented me. It wasn't being imposed on me based on what I assumed others gave. It has been liberating ever since. Always give proportionally. Don't settle for less. Give until it feels good!

The Rt. Rev. Robert W. Ihloff
Bishop of Maryland, Retired

Proportional Giving—A Percentage   G 15

The size of your gift isn't as important as what it represents to you. Someone may give a million dollars, which might seem like a lot, but might only be a drop in the bucket given their worth. This is why Jesus tells the story of the widow's mite (Mark 12:41–44). The correct way to measure any gift is by what it represents to the giver: Is it sacrificial? Is it meaningful? Or is it, in reality, puny?

If you think of your gift as a percentage of your income, you can measure your thankfulness. Figure it out. What proportion of your income is your gift? Then ask the question, "Am I pleased to be giving such a percentage?" If the answer is yes, it will make you feel good; if the answer is no, you may want to raise the amount. Let your gift be the measure of your thankfulness; let it speak your investment and commitment to the ministry or cause.

The Rt. Rev. Robert W. Ihloff
Bishop of Maryland, Retired

Proportional Giving—A Way to Give   G 16

How can I feel good about giving less than I want to give? This problem besets many people in our society. I'm reminded of a parishioner who came to me in tears. She was single and had lost her job; she had come to say she could not fulfill her church pledge. She was a proportional giver, giving about 8 percent of her income to the church. Clearly she could not continue to give so generous an amount since she would be living on unemployment. We talked about what her new income would be and she decided she could still give 8 percent. The new dollar amount of her pledge was much smaller, but she was actually giving just as generously. When she found a new job months later, she raised the dollar amount of her giving, keeping the same percent. Through it all, she felt good about her gift and was a cheerful giver. One of the great things about giving a proportion is it frees us from the tyranny of the dollar amount. We need to share such stories with good people who are on fixed incomes or are experiencing tragedies. They can still be generous and feel good about giving less.

The Rt. Rev. Robert W. Ihloff
Bishop of Maryland, Retired

Proportionate Giving   G 17

Does the inequality in this country bother you? Does it color your daily life? Data tells us that inequality is huge. The top 1 percent in America owns more than the bottom 90 percent. The social balance between groups is seriously disrupted. When so few have so much, the rest of us experience more suspicion and distrust. We are the wealthiest country in the world and the most skewed in distribution of ownership.

It is difficult for individuals to respond to that imbalance personally. We cannot erase differences between us in terms of ownership, but a society where those differences seem unfair or unbalanced creates stress. Inequality affects our caring for each other; and how we care depends, partly, on the kind of social service networks that help those in need. If the networks fray, then we all become more anxious. Jesus said it was difficult for the rich man to pass through the eye of the needle—difficult, but not impossible.

One small action we can take involves our own resources. How do we manage what we have with an eye on a larger picture? Using our money in a disciplined way helps to counter the pressures of unfairness and of consumerism. Proportional giving is a strategy to help us extend our resources beyond our individual needs. Giving 3 percent, 5 percent, 8 percent, or 10 percent becomes a habit that informs the rest of our spending. The important point is to commit to a specific level of generosity, integrating it into our everyday spending patterns.

Americans have a lot of stuff in our lives: full closets, full larders. We embody that favorite phrase of car dealers: we come fully loaded. How much is enough? It is a question to ponder.

Dr. Mary Blair
Chair, Stewardship Team, Cathedral of the Incarnation,
Baltimore, Maryland

Radical Giving   G 18

Jesus said to [the young man], "If you wish to be perfect, go, sell your possessions, and give the money to the poor, and you will have treasure in heaven; then come, follow me." When the young man heard this word, he went away grieving, for he had many possessions. (Matt. 19:21–22)

Public Christianity in America seems to tend toward biblical literalism. I am talking about the folks we hear on television and in popular culture. They pick this or that passage and present it—sometimes like a fortune-cookie saying—as a way to live. While I do think the Bible offers us guidance for how to live, I think we have to look at the big picture, including, yes, some pesky bits we'd like to ignore.

Matthew 19:21 feels like a pesky bit many Christians would like to ignore. Sign-toting protesters never put this on in gaudy colors and shout it out. But there it is: red-letter teaching from Jesus. If you want to follow me, he says, you need to sell your stuff and give the money to the poor. Funny how those who take the Bible literally never cite this passage.

For most of us, our stuff becomes a barrier between God and us. We love our stuff. We like to get more stuff. I'm sure I'm not the only one who decides, occasionally, to buy stuff I don't need instead of giving that money to someone else who needs it more than I do. Jesus is inviting us to be radical. Few of us will have the courage to do what he suggests. But maybe we can get glimpses of the glory of God in our lives as we learn to care more about God and less about stuff.

The Rev. Canon Scott Gunn
Executive Director, Forward Movement, Cincinnati, Ohio

Reconciliation and a Gift   G 19

After I received a call to serve a rebuilding mission in 2010, a retired priest who had found a home in the same church wrote to say that he was leaving because his theology did not support the ordination of women. He wished me well. Believing that his absence would signal a great loss for us all, I wrote back to ask if we could have lunch before he made a final decision. He agreed. That lunch with one twenty-six years my senior began a friendship now seven years strong. Although he and I have rarely discussed women's ordination, we marvel at how our Anglo-Catholic beliefs dovetail over the generations. It was an honor to plan a celebration of the fiftieth anniversary of his ordination in 2012, to which many who represented fruits of his five decades of priesthood came.

Now that our mission has doubled in size, there is no doubt that we owe much to God's grace, hard-working lay leaders, and the collaborative model of clergy leadership that he, another retired priest, and I together offer.

On my last birthday, this priest gave me a stole that had been made for his ordination in 1962. The red Chinese silk decorated with woven 24-carat gold tau crosses have weathered well over fifty-five years. He wrote, "I have had occasions to wear this stole for ordinations and Masses of the Holy Spirit. I hope if you should have such occasions to please send up a dart prayer on my behalf. Happy Birthday, and many, many more as you continue your very successful ministry." For this gift that symbolizes Christ's wellspring of reconciliation, bought by such a precious sacrifice, I am most grateful. And wear it I will, offering up more than a dart prayer of gratitude for its giver.

The Rev. Dr. Laura Sheridan-Campbell
Vicar, Holy Cross Church, Carlsbad, California

Seafarers Center—
Glad and Generous Heart   G 20

Port chaplains often transport seafarers ashore for a change of scenery, a few hasty errands, or worship. Other authorized security escorts who accompany foreign crew members from the gangway to the terminal gate may charge steep fees—but we provide this service for free.

One day, I offered to take several Filipino crew members ashore. They worked on a coal ship, and this was their only chance in months to set foot on land. When we got to the terminal gate, there was a problem with their paperwork. Though it wasn't their fault, they lost their chance to go out, so I had to drive them back to the vessel. But what almost had me in tears was that, despite never getting outside the gate, these generous men still thanked me and wanted to donate for gasoline. Their wages are much smaller than most Americans' wages, yet they still "give thanks in all circumstances" (cf. 1 Thess. 5:18). Thank all of you who support our Seafarers Ministry throughout our world.

The Rev. Mary Davisson
Executive Director/Port Chaplain, Baltimore International
Seafarers' Center

Seafarers—Tithe   G 21

As a port chaplain, I have spent many hours sitting in a passenger cruise terminal interacting with crew members lucky enough to have a short break while in port. Some have had questions about Baltimore, some have requested free Bibles, and some have just wanted to chat. One day, an assistant waiter from a cruise ship handed me a fat envelope full of money labeled "tithe" and asked me to "give it to the church."

"Which church?" I asked.

Amused by my question, he replied, "Any church! It's my tithe!"

"Any church." Not the one that sings his favorite hymns. Not even Protestant or Catholic. Just any church. Truly, that hard-working assistant waiter had a "glad and generous heart." (cf. Acts. 2.46) Thank all of you who support our Seafarers Ministry throughout our world.

The Rev. Mary Davisson
Executive Director/Port Chaplain, Baltimore International
Seafarers' Center

The Smallest of Seeds   G 22

Mark 6:30–34

Osceola McCarty was an African-American woman born in poverty in 1908 in rural Mississippi. When just a sixth grader in Hattiesburg, Mississippi, her caretaker aunt became ill, so she quit school in order to provide homecare. She later became a washerwoman, taking in white people's laundry in her home for small change. During all those years, she put aside a portion of her meager earnings every week, even opening a savings account at a local bank. As bank personnel noticed the growing funds, they began to assist her with financial planning.

In 1995 she walked into the president's office at the University of Southern Mississippi to announce a bequest of $150,000, pledged in gratitude for her own son's education there, and which she asked to be used for other African-American students who could not afford to attend college.

Now you understand why on that day the university president drew a deep breath, realizing all that this gift represented. Now you understand why Osceola McCarty drew global attention for her stunning generosity—and why, when she died in 1999, she was most famous benefactor in that school's history. And now you also understand—no matter one's station in life, level of education, or income—how faith the size of a mustard seed can change the world.

The Rt. Rev. Joe Goodwin Burnett
Tenth Bishop of Nebraska, 2003–2011

Suggested uses for the above meditation: Easter Season; the season after Pentecost

Section VI

Special Occasion Meditations

Acolytes   SO 1

Acolytes are those who serve the priest-pastor at the altar. These are generally young people, boys and girls, who faithfully act as crucifer, candle bearers, banner carriers, and assist in preparing for communion. In some congregations adults serve in this capacity.

———

This morning we are installing N_____, N_____, and N_____ into our acolyte guild. We will be giving each of them a cross to symbolize the Lord Jesus Christ they serve. We give thanks this morning for all our acolytes. They enrich our worship and are much appreciated. They practice their stewardship by giving of their time and abilities to serve. Thank you, too, who faithfully give your money week by week to support this ministry.

OR

Today we celebrate our acolytes. These young people and adults give of their time each Sunday, acting as crucifers, candle bearers, banner carriers, and serving our priest to prepare for communion. They are practicing their stewardship as they serve, and thanks to all who give generously to provide moving worship every Sunday.

Adult Choir   SO 2

> O sing to the LORD a new song; sing to the LORD, all the earth.
> (Ps. 96:1)

Our adult choir makes a joyful sound each week because your gifts provide funds for purchasing single anthems or books with inspiring choral music to uplift our hearts. The congregation is grateful to the choir for the message only music can convey. The choir appreciates the reward they receive from learning these anthems, for the restorative joy they feel singing them, and for the fellowship that results from their hard work. Anyone who has sung in a choral group knows the bond that is created by singing ensemble music and how the text clothed in melody comes alive in their hearts. Thank you for making all this possible through your pledge to support our adult choir.

Constance Hegarty
Retired Organist and Choir Director,
Windsor Locks, Connecticut

Advent and Christmas
with St. Nicholas   SO 3

As we enter the season of Advent and look forward to the Feast of the Incarnation, we remember Bishop Nicholas of Myra. His generosity toward the less fortunate and his love of children have become legendary. At this time of year we are bombarded by suggestions of how our gifts at Christmas can make recipients happy. Let us consider as well what good our gifts can do this season. Thank you for giving so generously during this season to support the [*name of specific program*]. Your gifts have made a difference!

The Rev. Elizabeth Rust Masterson
Rector (retired), St. Nicholas' Church, Newark, Delaware

American Friends of the Episcopal Diocese of Jerusalem—Ahli Arab Hospital   SO 4

Gaza is a place like no other: an open-air prison where war after war has left rubble where homes, schools, and workplaces used to be. The Ahli Arab Hospital is the last full-service Christian hospital in Gaza, bravely maintaining a Christian witness. Families have no money to pay for services and the hospital can only stay open with significant support from donors around the world. Erratic electrical power, no potable water, equipment breakdowns, and chronic medication shortages make quality care challenging for the staff. We met a woman who had given birth an hour before, but who welcomed strangers into her room. We asked why she had chosen Ahli, which charges a small fee, rather than the free government hospital down the road. She said she wanted her child to enter the world surrounded by dignity and respect. She expressed gratitude to the hospital and the kindly staff. Financial support from donors to the American Friends of the Episcopal Diocese of Jerusalem helps keep the doors of this hospital open, Christian witness in a volatile place. This new mother and AFEDJ thank you for this critical support.

Anne K. Lynn
President, American Friends of the Episcopal Diocese of Jerusalem

American Friends of the Episcopal Diocese of Jerusalem—Episcopal Vocational School   SO 5

Yousef hated school. When he failed every course at his high school, his father went to the parish priest in Ramallah, West Bank, seeking support.

Unemployment in the West Bank among young men is extremely high and, with nothing to do and no future, many make bad decisions. But Fr. Fadi offered more than a shoulder. He suggested that Yousef try for a scholarship to attend the Episcopal Vocational School. Academics are combined with culinary and hospitality training, preparing students for jobs in restaurants and hotels. Yousef found his calling. He graduated at the top of his class and was offered a well-paying job with a future. The American Friends of the Episcopal Diocese of Jerusalem found a scholarship donor for Yousef. The donation of the money to fund this scholarship offers an example to all who would offer hope to those students struggling in our Holy Land. Thank you!

Anne K. Lynn
President, American Friends of the Episcopal Diocese of
Jerusalem

American Friends of the Episcopal Diocese of Jerusalem—Judean Desert   SO 6

When Jesus went into the wilderness for forty days, he went to the Judean desert a few hours walk from the bustling city of Jerusalem. It is a uniquely barren land of cliffs, sand, and heat. Several ancient monasteries are literally carved into the sides of the hills, with caves or niches dug out where hermits of old lived solitary lives of prayer and privation. We learned that monks lowered baskets of food to the hermits. If the basket was left untouched for a few days, it was assumed that the hermit had died. That was it. No ceremony, no family advised. The monks just moved on to provide food to another cave. These hermits lived lives of overwhelming humility, made complete by continuous prayer. May we gain the clarity to know God's will for us and the gratitude that comes with that certainty.

Anne K. Lynn
President, American Friends of the Episcopal Diocese
of Jerusalem

American Friends of the Episcopal Diocese of Jerusalem— Mount of the Beatitudes   SO 7

The Mount of the Beatitudes is a gently sloping hill, overlooking the Sea of Galilee. It is dislocating to stand amid the tall grass and wildflowers and think that Jesus might have stood in that exact place, preaching some portion of some of the most well-known words in scripture. It is no longer a story in a book from long ago and far away in that moment. The gospel becomes real—a truth. Jesus's words define discipleship for us in ways that broke all the rules of the time. The Sermon on the Mount is the new covenant distilled to its essence. For any pilgrim, gratitude for the chance to stand in that place lasts a lifetime. We can show our gratitude for this opportunity or other opportunities that enliven our faith by generous giving to the ministries whose importance stems from Jesus's teachings.

Anne K. Lynn
President, American Friends of the Episcopal Diocese of Jerusalem

Baptism   SO 8

Baptisms in the Episcopal Church are normally done on certain feast days and other Sundays that are convenient to the families. They are done as the first half of the service, followed by the Eucharist. In the Episcopal Church we have "The Presentation" (during which the names of the candidates for baptism are announced) followed by "The Baptism." This question is put to the entire congregation as part of the Presentation: "Will you who witness these vows do all in your power to support these persons in their life in Christ?" The people respond with a resounding, "We will" (BCP, 303).

This morning we are privileged to be here to welcome and be present for the baptism of N_____ and N_____. Baptism is the entrance into Christian discipleship. During our service we all were asked "Will you who witness these vows do all in your power to support these persons in their life in Christ?" I heard a resounding "We will." What does the "We will" mean as members of this church? It means we will be encouragers of these children as they grow and come of age in our congregation. We will respect them. Some among us will teach them the Christian faith in church school and all of us will be examples of how one lives the Christian life. It means that through our contributions to the church we will provide them with good church school materials, clean classrooms, a good youth program, and lively and meaningful worship. Thank you for saying "We will."

OR

Thank you for being here this morning as we commit ourselves to support these children in their life in Christ. Their parents and godparents promised "with God's help" to "be responsible for seeing the child you present is brought up in the Christian faith and life" (BCP, 302).

This means through the stewardship of our time, talents, abilities, and our money we will provide a place where these children will experience, by example, how one lives the Christian life. Thank you!

Bible Study   SO 9

Every (put in day) a group of our faithful church members meet to study scripture here at _____. We (they) gather together to learn about our faith, share insights, and grow our (their) understanding of the Bible. I want to thank all who give to support _____. You make it possible for us to meet and share our faith. Our church is a place that takes our Bible seriously, and all are always welcome.

Bishop's Visitation—Thank You!   SO 10

Saying thank you to the people who have made contributions is easy, and it works every time. Whenever I visit parishes I tell them, just before the offering, the exact amount of money they have given to the diocese in the past year. "Did you know that $_____ went from this church to support the wider mission of the Episcopal Church this past year? Thank you! Now let me tell you what your giving has done. . . ." I then highlight the good work of a few ministries that depend upon diocesan support, both near and far away.

Are the members of your church thanked publicly and frequently for what they are doing in stewardship? Nothing spurs more giving than genuine appreciation expressed for past giving. People need to know that they are making a difference.

The Rt. Rev. Eugene Taylor Sutton
Bishop, Episcopal Diocese of Maryland

Boy Scouts   SO 11

Every week here at _____ Boy Scout Troop # _____ meets here on (day, time). There are (number of boys in the troop) young men who attend faithfully as they learn camping skills, self-reliance, and how to live by the Boy Scout Oath. I want to thank you for your giving here at _____. Your generosity enhances our community because we sponsor Troop # _____ (or provide Troop #_____ a safe place to meet). This is one of the ways our congregation positively impacts our community. Young men are being shaped by our outstanding troop and learning to live by the Boy Scout Oath. We can all benefit from their motto "Be Prepared." Today, on Scout Sunday, we honor all the Boy Scouts in our congregation and community.

Campus Ministry—The Hidden
Work of the Gospel   SO 12

> Complete possession is proved only by giving. All you are unable
> to give possesses you.
>
> —Andre Gide

College students and young adults can be an invisible generation in
many churches: they go away to college, join the military, move away for
work, or simply don't seem to be around. This can make many congregations anxious: Where are they? How can we get them back? Campus
and young adult ministries help to make space for young adults who
are asking urgent questions of meaning and identity and vocation. They
depend on the generosity of all in the church to do the work of the gospel
in the places where young adults are found. Giving toward what we do,
yet not see, is the freedom at the heart of stewardship. Your contribution
demonstrates that freedom and your trust in that hidden, yet vital work.
Thank you.

The Rev. Stacy Alan
Chaplain, Brent House, the Episcopal Center at the
University of Chicago

Campus Ministry—Hundreds
of Beautiful Things   SO 13

> The world is full of hundreds of beautiful things we can never
> possibly have time to discover, and there is no time to be unkind
> or envious or ungenerous, and no sense in enslaving the mind
> to the trivialities of the moment. For you can be equal to the
> greatness of life only by marching with it; not by seeking love
> but by giving it, nor by seeking to be understood, but by learn-
> ing to understand.
>
> —Vivienne de Watteville (British travel
> writer and adventurer, 1900–1957)

One of the great delights of working on a college campus is being in a place in which there is always something new to discover: ideas and inventions, science and art, skills and facts. Hundreds of beautiful things, indeed. Ministry here is about celebrating those things—finding God in the beauty and complexity and struggles of the "life of the mind"—but it's also about learning a kind of spiritual discipline, one that explores this rich terrain with an open heart, not hoarding the knowledge for its own sake, but gathering it with the heart of a steward. Campus ministries are places where stewardship is learned for the whole of life; all that we receive, whether it is knowledge or skill or money, is to be offered generously for the good of the world. We are grateful to those who have opened their hearts and supported our work: they have contributed in their own way to the treasure trove of beautiful things.

The Rev. Stacy Alan
Chaplain, Brent House, the Episcopal Center at the
University of Chicago

Campus Ministry—
Send Heralds Forth   SO 14

Send heralds forth to bear the message glorious;
give of thy wealth to speed them on their way;
pour out thy soul for them in prayer victorious
till God shall bring his kingdom's joyful day.
Publish glad tidings: tidings of peace,
tidings of Jesus, redemption and release.

—Mary Ann Thomson, "O Zion, haste,"
#539 from Hymnal 1982[1]

I often compare campus and young adult ministry to the old-fashioned notion of the "mission field." Here we enter a "foreign" territory with

---

deep respect and humility, watching and listening carefully for signs of God already working there, asking where we can be of service, proclaiming God's love in Christ by word and deed. And, just as in the days when this hymn was written, we depend on the generosity of those at "home" to be "sped on our way." God is indeed working on campus. The generous stewardship of those in parishes helps us to follow God's call.

The Rev. Stacy Alan
Chaplain, Brent House, the Episcopal Center at the
University of Chicago

Campus Ministry—Where Are We to Get Enough   SO 15

> The disciples said to him, "Where are we to get enough bread in the desert to feed so great a crowd?" Jesus asked them, "How many loaves have you?" They said, "Seven, and a few small fish." (Matt. 15:33–34)

For many undergraduates, college is their first time having to figure out how to be stewards of their own resources. "Where are we to get enough?" is often asked about time, money, sleep, research, internships, and, for some, even food. Our campus ministries model Jesus's stewardship by helping them ask each other, "What do we have?" and encouraging them to share out of what seems scarce, trusting that God's abundance will be revealed. These become habits of generosity that our students will take beyond their college years into the rest of their lives. Thank you for modeling your own generous answers to Jesus's question and by showing that there is, indeed, enough.

The Rev. Stacy Alan
Chaplain, Brent House, the Episcopal Center at the
University of Chicago

Capital Campaign—Gratitude   SO 16

Please accept our sincere gratitude for your generous support of our capital campaign. Your sacrificial pledge will provide the necessary financial support required to address immediate parish needs and will set a model for fellow parishioners to follow. Indeed, it will help to draw all of us beyond ourselves and motivate us to reflect on the graciousness of God.

Robert B. Rice
Principal and Managing Director, CCS Fundraising

Capital Campaign—
Thank You for Your Pledge   SO 17

Thank you for your generous support to our capital campaign. As you know, this effort will enable us to fulfill the vision for our essential facilities during this pivotal time in our parish's history. Your pledge provided much needed support to our campaign and helped to ensure our success. We are so very grateful. Many thanks for your continued commitment to our church. We are proud of how our parish has stepped forward to provide gifts now and for generations to follow. Please pray for our continued success as we move forward together.

Robert B. Rice
Principal and Managing Director, CCS Fundraising

Children in Worship   SO 18

Children are often described as our future. I reject that proposal. Children in our church are our present. They bring life, hope, and energy to our congregations. I was taught in seminary that Christianity is only one generation away from extinction.

This morning I want to thank our parents of our wonderful children. Our parents faithfully bring their children to our worship and lovingly care for them and, by example, teach them how to behave in church. I thank you all for your patience and love of our children. I thank you all for your faithful stewardship and giving that enable us to have a welcoming church.

OR

This morning we give thanks for the children of our parish. We are indeed blessed to have them as active members of our congregation. They bring life to our church and remind us all that we once were children, Thank you all for supporting our children's ministries by being teachers and by generously giving so our children have clean, well-equipped classrooms with the finest church school materials. You are the reason we have so many wonderful children in our congregation. Thank you.

Church School   SO 19

We have a fine church school to educate our children in how we live our lives as Christians in what is often a troubled and confusing world. We give thanks for our teachers who give their time and talents to teach our children. We thank all members who support and respect our children and who warmly welcome them into our life as a loving congregation. We thank you for your generous offerings that enable us to provide wonderful church school materials and clean and bright classrooms.

OR

Every Sunday our parents bring their children to our church school and to worship with us. They are embracing the promise they and the children's godparents made at their children's baptism when they were asked, "Will you be responsible for seeing the child they present is brought up in the Christian faith and life?"

The parents and godparents responded, "I will, with God's help." I thank all of you who welcome our children and, through faithful stewardship, who enable our parents and godparents to fulfill their promises made to God.

Church School—End of Year   SO 20

This Sunday we are celebrating our children, youth, and the teachers of our church school. We have had a good year due to the faithfulness of our parents who have brought their children to church week by week. Our teachers have planned their lessons and programs well. And you, the congregation, have welcomed our children to worship. You have given generously to create a congregation that lives out God's abundant generosity. We know our children not only represent our future, but they also bring life to our congregation right now!

OR

Today we celebrate our church school as we come to the end of our program year. We want to thank our teachers. We have a carnation for each of them—our way of saying thank you. We also have a wonderful special cake for our teachers, children, parents, and the entire congregation as an expression of our gratitude. You are all responsible for creating an atmosphere of welcoming generosity and abundance for our children. Your generous giving makes all this possible.

Confirmation—Youth   SO 21

This (Next) Sunday Bishop _____ will be here to confirm (number) of our youth. They have been preparing through an excellent program call J2A, Journey to Adulthood. Each of our youth has a sponsor and will be presented to the bishop by their parents and their sponsor. I want to thank their teachers and you, the members of our congregation, for encouraging and supporting them in their journey. Your generous giving has enabled them to experience lively worship and the best of a compassionate Christian community. When the bishop lays his/her hands on them, please smile; you made it possible.

OR

Bishop _____ is here today to confirm (number) young persons of our congregation. I am so thankful you are here to support them in this important milestone in their spiritual journey. I want to thank their parents who have brought them here week by week, their teachers who have prepared them, and you who are here today to witness their commitment to Jesus Christ. Thank you all for your generous stewardship, that provides a place of learning, a place of worship and compassionate community, and a place of generosity and abundance.

Consider Your Heavens   SO 22

The psalmist said, "When I consider your heavens, the work of your fingers, the moon and the stars which you have set in their courses, what is man that you should be mindful of him? the son of man, that you should seek him out? You have made him but little lower than the angels, and you adorn him with glory and honor." (Ps. 8:4–6, BCP)

It is a marvelous universe, an awesome creation and we have evolving comprehension of its glory, its needs, and our responsibility. The psalmist hinted at that in the next verse: "You give him mastery over the works of your hands; you put all things under his feet." In keeping with our growth through the Christian proclamation that we are in partnership with our Creator, we more clearly understand that we are stewards of this planet, with the power to enhance its beauty or shred it of its livability.

There are many creative ways to be good stewards. Through the body of Christ, the church, we have the opportunity to be his hands, his feet, his architects, his sojourners of the planet and beyond, as well as his love for those in any need or distress. May the Lord accompany our work in the vineyard to God's honor and glory. Amen.

The Rev. Stephen Parker
Author, *Bridges: Embracing Faith and Science*, retired
Chaplain, Salisbury School, Salisbury, Connecticut

Diocesan Convention   SO 23

This coming Saturday, our clergy and our elected Convention delegate (delegates) will be attending our diocesan convention. We thank them for their generous stewardship in giving of their time and abilities to represent our congregation in the larger church. We ask your prayers as these delegates vote and make decisions affecting not only our church, but all the churches in our diocese. Thank all of you who generously give week by week to enable our congregation to support our diocesan ministries. We pray that we will represent you well.

OR

In the Episcopal Church (your denomination) we have an annual gathering of all clergy and lay delegates elected by their congregations to conduct business and make decisions for our diocese (your regional body). We thank our lay delegates who said yes to go and represent us. We will meet this Saturday at _____. Please keep us in your prayers as we make decisions affecting our life together as a diocese (your regional body). Thank you for your faithful stewardship that enables us to financially support our diocesan ministries.

Diocesan Support   SO 24

Being an Episcopalian (name your own denomination) means we are part of a larger church body beyond our local congregation or parish. In the Episcopal Church we have dioceses, normally a geographical area named after a state or city. We also belong to the Episcopal Church, which is headquartered in New York City. Every Episcopal parish is expected to financially support their diocese, and each diocese is expected to financially support the Episcopal Church.

Today, we want to thank you for your faithful giving to our church. On behalf of our Bishop _____, thank you for sharing your gifts, given week by week to our parish. For every dollar given, we share a small portion of it with our diocese to support ministries beyond our congregation that we could not manage to do on our own. (Give examples.) In turn, our diocese gives a portion of the contributions they receive to support the ministries of the Episcopal Church. (Give examples.) When you read and hear about the wonderful ministries of our diocese and of the Episcopal Church, feel good. You helped to make them happen. Bishop _____ and I say, "Thank you."

OR

Today we want to thank you for your financial support of our diocese. We, as a congregation, will give $_____ this year to support the work of our diocese and the Episcopal Church in the greater ministry beyond our congregation. (Add specific ministries in your diocese that are changing lives.) Your giving makes a difference not only in our church, but it also makes a difference in changing lives throughout our diocese, the United States, and to the world. Thank you.

Electronic Giving—EFT   SO 25

We are thankful to those who give using electronic funds transfer, or EFT. As we move through the year, most of our expenses remain the same, but our income fluctuates. Particularly in the summer when many people travel, it can be a challenge to pay our bills. Having a steady stream of giving throughout the year, regardless of whether or not people are in church on a given weekend, helps us to fulfill God's mission for our church. For this, we are immensely grateful.

Julia Pearson
Canon for Evangelism, Cathedral of the Incarnation,
Baltimore, Maryland

Electronic Giving—Online SO 26

Thank you to those who give to our church using our website or other online source. In this day and age where so few people carry cash and checks, the fact that you make the effort to take a minute to go online and give is wonderful. Your gift enables us to further God's mission for our church, and we are appreciative.

Julia Pearson
Canon for Evangelism, Cathedral of the Incarnation,
Baltimore, Maryland

Environment SO 27

We thank God for our beautiful planet Earth. And we recognize that nature makes our lives better. We need nature and nature needs us. No matter where we live, we depend on nature every day. We recognize that healthy lands and waters are the foundation of a prosperous society, and that practicing good stewardship of the Earth and its many resources is honoring God.

We pray for a world where the diversity of life thrives, and where people act to conserve nature for its own sake, and for its ability to fulfill our needs and enrich our lives.

Greg Sharkey
Senior Philanthropy Advisor, The Nature Conservancy

Episcopal Migration Ministries—
Love and Grace SO 28

Do not withhold good from those to whom it is due, when it is
in your power to do it. (Prov. 3:27)

I've given out of obligation before, without much thought. It was required, I believed. My tithe was another monthly expense. I wrote the rent check. I wrote the church check. I moved on to the water bill.

Income in, expenses out. I have recently had occasion to reevaluate this utilitarian approach. As Episcopal Migration Ministries has received checks from dioceses across the country in response to the refugee crisis, I have been struck by the deeply personal nature of true generosity. The giver witnessed deprivation and responded in kind, as the writer of Proverb 3:27 instructs. The gift came from one and is going to another. Because of a gift from Baltimore, an arriving refugee family has a hot meal and warm beds. Because of a gift from Houston, a refugee has an interpreter for her doctor's visit. Because of a gift from New York, a single man fleeing for his life and leaving family behind now takes English classes with a group of others. The giver and receiver may never meet, but they are bound together by the deeply personal nature of the act—by this generosity and the grace inherent in its reception. And these are the things—these personal acts—that give breath and life to our faith and that keep the world spinning on its axis in the end. John writes that God is Love. I experience this Love in action, in the space between people, even those who may never meet. May these generous gifts and this Love and Grace abound. And may it begin in me.

Our thanks to the generous giving of our dioceses that make this ministry possible.

Heather Joseph
Senior Program Manager, Foundational Programs,
Episcopal Migration Ministries

Episcopal Migration Ministries— Welcome the Stranger   SO 29

Love is a choice we make; it's an expression of our faith. Most of us share that love with those closest to us: our families, friends, and maybe even our colleagues. Making the choice to share love with those we may never meet is harder . . . and yet, that is what we do each time we make the faith-filled choice to give of our time, talent, and treasure. Each time we do that, we proclaim that we have chosen love.

Bearing witness to love is the source of my faith. My work at Episcopal Migration Ministries (EMM) welcoming refugees has been a topic of political debate lately. It would be easy to lose faith in this time when humanity seems to be so hostile and broken, when voices of those in power are asking us to turn our backs on the world's most vulnerable—neighbors we haven't yet met, but neighbors all the same.

My faith teaches me that love is stronger than hate, and that even the smallest gifts—time, treasure, talent—are acts of love that restore hope. At EMM, we often receive letters and phone calls thanking us for our work and asking how to help. These small acts of love carry me; they buoy me up. They restore hope for all of us who serve the church through EMM's ministry of refugee resettlement, and they further encourage and share love with the refugee women, children, and men whom we welcome to safety as our newest neighbors.

And so, we thank you for your prayers, for your gifts of time, talent, and treasure, for the pledge you make to your local congregation, for the offering you place in the plate. These gifts share the Good News—in your congregation, in your community, and with those whom you may never meet. These gifts share the Good News of God's love with those who have fled persecution and violence and seek nothing more than to rebuild their lives in safety and hope. Your faithful stewardship is part of this life-saving ministry of hope.

Amanda Beyer
Senior Program Officer, Episcopal Migration Ministries

Episcopal Refugee and Immigrant Center Alliance—Church Tithing   SO 30

Tithing for outreach is common practice in many churches, but tithing at a significant level and annually directing a large portion of that sum to develop and support a church's own ministry, linked to its traditions, current membership, and local community, is unusual. It shouldn't be! It creates a powerful energy within the congregation, inspiring newcomers and long-term members alike to take the risks and make the individual contributions that reflect their commitment to God and the church where they worship. Stewardship also reflects the soul of a church, highlights its history, and becomes a beacon for the spiritual path of the congregation as a whole. Thank you for brightening this beacon.

Betty Symington
Executive Director, ERICA—Episcopal Refugee and
Immigrant Center Alliance, Baltimore, MD

Episcopal Refugee and Immigrant Center Alliance— Congregation Tithing   SO 31

Here at our church, we tithe ourselves as a congregation, setting aside 10 percent of total annual pledges for outreach. I am not sure when this practice began, but it has allowed us to support numerous worthy initiatives while at the same time creating, nurturing, and sustaining our own: ERICA, the Episcopal Refugee and Immigrant Center Alliance. ERICA is a unique outreach ministry that provides assistance for refugees and asylum seekers rebuilding their lives in our local community. Thank you for welcoming the stranger through your commitment to the Cathedral.

Betty Symington
Executive Director, ERICA—Episcopal Refugee and
Immigrant Center Alliance, Baltimore, MD

Episcopal Refugee and Immigrant Center Alliance—History   SO 32

The Episcopal Refugee and Immigrant Center Alliance (ERICA) began in 2001, when asylum seekers from Liberia who were members of the church brought their stories to the attention of their congregation. Its roots go deeper yet, as the church participated in the direct sponsorship of refugee families when the U.S. refugee resettlement program began in the 1980s. Today, our program receives about one-third of its budget from the Cathedral and raises the rest from individual donations, small grants, and events. It is part of the fabric of this congregation. Thank you for embellishing this fabric through your stewardship.

Betty Symington
Executive Director, ERICA—Episcopal Refugee and
Immigrant Center Alliance, Baltimore, MD

Episcopal Refugee and Immigrant Center Alliance—Let Your Sibling In   SO 33

One Sunday in our church, the sermon focused on what it meant to be open to change. We were asked to remember a recent experience that had changed us. A friend told me what immediately came to mind was her family's decision to host an asylum seeker in their home. It completely changed her perspective on immigration; no longer only a partisan issue, it had become a complex web of compelling personal stories of people with profoundly different journeys from her own, but whom she now saw as folks much like herself. She had not anticipated the comfort of new connection and understanding.

When I sing the fraction hymn at communion, I think of my friend. We are quite familiar with acting upon the words of Jesus, "In remembrance of me, heal the sick; in remembrance of me, feed the poor." And if we take literally rather than figuratively the third instruction, "In remembrance of me, open the door and let your brother [or sister] in, let them in," we will be taking a particularly bold step. We will make ourselves vulnerable, we will expose ourselves, but we will also learn, connect, and become confident welcomers.

It is helpful to think of stewardship in a similar way. It is hard to admit that when we give money to church we feel a little more vulnerable, we worry that we have less of something we might need. But if we accept this vulnerability, if we embrace it as both real and natural, then we are opening the door to let Jesus and others in. Thank you for opening the door.

Betty Symington
Executive Director, ERICA—Episcopal Refugee and
Immigrant Center Alliance, Baltimore, MD

Episcopal Relief and
Development Sunday   SO 34

At the 2009 General Convention of the Episcopal Church, Lent was officially designated as a time to encourage the whole church to remember and support the life-saving work of Episcopal Relief and Development. Congregations are invited to commemorate Episcopal Relief and Development Sunday on the first Sunday of Lent, or another convenient Sunday during the Lenten season. Given the call to prayerfully support the work of Episcopal Relief and Development, I invite you to meditate on our mandate that comes from Jesus's words found in Matthew 25:37–40:

> Lord, when was it that we saw you hungry and gave you food, or thirsty and gave you something to drink? And when was it that we saw you a stranger and welcomed you. . . ? And when was it that we saw you sick or in prison and visited you? . . . Truly I tell you, just as you did it to one of the least of these who are members of my family, you did it to me.

Each day, in one way or another, we encounter people who are hungry, thirsty, estranged, sick, or imprisoned. Most of us have choices as to how we can respond. We can respond with our head—make a donation to a local feeding program, schedule time to volunteer at a homeless shelter, or advocate for better government policy. All are important responses. We also need to make time to respond with our hearts. Responding with our hearts usually takes more time than we are willing to spend, so we retreat and find an excuse. Or we risk being vulnerable ourselves. On this day that we remember the ministry of Episcopal

Relief and Development, how can we be both head and heart Christians when it comes to Matthew 25? Episcopal Relief and Development is grateful for your prayers and support during Lent.

Robert W. Radtke
President, Episcopal Relief and Development,
New York, New York

Episcopal Service Corps—
Finding and Affirming Gifts   SO 35

It was revealed to them that they were serving not themselves but you, in regard to the things that have now been announced to you through those who brought you good news by the Holy Spirit sent from heaven—things into which angels long to look! (1 Pet. 1:12)

Episcopal Service Corps members come from all over our country, and even from overseas. They are in their twenties. Most have recently graduated from college, or have decided to take a year off. Some graduated a few years ago and have heard the Spirit in new ways. They come for a year of service, to live intentionally in community, and to discern and find tools for their own next steps as faithful young people growing into adults. Most find gifts they never knew—perseverance, patience, courage, and flexibility. Most affirm gifts they knew or suspected they already had received—generosity, openheartedness, thoughtfulness, faithfulness. These they give away freely to those in most need, to the lost, and to the marginalized. They discover that strangers become friends: housemates they have never met before their arrival, neighbors who live nearby in houses, and in doorways and on the streets. We give thanks for those who have given their year of service and faith over the years in cities and towns, camps and churches, shelters and other service sites in over twenty-five dioceses across the United States since our network became more formal in 2009. In their year, Corps members announce the Good News by their very presence. They certainly surprise themselves and perhaps even surprise the angels. This gift they give of themselves is possible only by your gifts of money, prayers, time. Here are links to some of our stories: http://episcopalservicecorps.org/stories/ and http://www.escmaryland.org/stories-from-the-gileads/.

The Rev. Canon Jan Hamill
Director, Episcopal Service Corps, Maryland

Episcopal Service Corps— How to Take God Seriously   SO 36

> How can I stand up before GOD and show proper respect to the high God? Should I bring an armload of offerings topped off with yearling calves? Would GOD be impressed with thousands of rams, with buckets and barrels of olive oil? Would he be moved if I sacrificed my firstborn child, my precious baby, to cancel my sin? But he's already made it plain how to live, what to do, what GOD is looking for in men and women. It's quite simple: Do what is fair and just to your neighbor, be compassionate and loyal in your love, and don't take yourself too seriously—take God seriously. (Micah 6:6–8, The Message)

How to take God seriously? Take yourself seriously, but not too much! The gift of laughter is probably the most important discovery that Episcopal Service Corps members make during their year of service and faith, whether it's in Baltimore; Boston; Steamboat Springs; Seattle; Washington, DC; Waialua; or one of the other Episcopal Service Corps programs in our network. Everyone comes with some sense of justice and eagerness to change the world in ways large and small, and even to be changed themselves. They learn to live into our seven core values: prayer, service, network, leadership, justice, community, and vocation. Often, though, to live intentionally in a household community of those who once were strangers is probably the hardest part of their year. And that usually requires a large dose of laughter. These young adults come with a variety of standards for sharing space, food, even cleanliness.

Some arrive never having shared a bedroom, much less cleaned a shared bathroom. They often discover God is not impressed with fancy degrees and awards or amazing semesters abroad in college, but rather how the gifts of fairness, kindness, and laughter are shared with those around us. That is yet one more way in which God's justice is done. Thank you for the ways in which you support this gift of a year of service—your prayers, your money, your time, and your laughter, too. Find us on Instagram and Twitter at @ESC, on Facebook, and on the web at www .episcopalservicecorps.org.

The Rev. Canon Jan Hamill
Director, Episcopal Service Corps, Maryland

EYE—Episcopal Youth Event SO 37
Psalm 42:1–6, 8

The 2017 Episcopal Youth Event will be the fifth time I have had the chance to take this life-changing pilgrimage. Youth in the modern world are frequently in a place of despair. The world seems so finite to them. A social situation can seem like the end of the world, or something truly awful happens and they cannot see a life after the tragedy. Their souls thirst for refreshment.

EYE is a chance for the youth, adults, and the church to have their souls refreshed. Each young person I have seen attend has come back assured that God is calling them by name. When 1,500 people are gathered together in community, it changes lives. The youth who have a chance to be part of a thriving faith-filled experience like EYE have a small glimpse of what the world could look like if we all truly worked to love one another as Christ loved us.

Having attended both as a youth and an adult, I can attest to how radically this community inspires everything from breakfast to choosing to spend a year in Episcopal Service Corps or the Young Adult Service Corps. EYE may be compacted into a small time frame, but it has a life-long impact on all who experience it.

Let us pray:

Loving Creator, you gave us a wide range of emotions. Some of them give us cause to pause or run in fear. Help us to know that you are always with us. Your presence is a comfort in the times of darkness and a beacon for following the call you set before us. Be in our hearts, minds, and souls as we build community all around the world in your name. Amen.

Thanks to everyone who supports our young people in our parish and diocese. Your generous giving makes a difference in our young people's lives.

Kate Riley
Diocesan Youth Missioner, The Episcopal Diocese of
Maryland

Facebook   SO 38

The late Rev. Terry Parsons, former stewardship officer of the Episcopal Church, said, "Show me your checkbook register and I can tell you what's important to you." Today we can say the same thing about your Facebook posts or your Twitter feed. Imagine looking for examples of how you're living out the gospel as you tell your story on social media. Would anyone find you doing what Jesus did? Would they see how you comfort the afflicted or feed the hungry and clothe the naked? Meredith Gould, who has been called an apostle to the Internet, paraphrased the words of Teresa of Avila for this century.

Christ has no online presence but yours. No blog, no Facebook page but yours. Yours are the tweets through which love touches this world. Yours are the posts through which the gospel is shared. Yours are the updates though which hope is revealed. Christ has no online presence but yours. No blog, no Facebook page but yours.[2]

---

2. Meredith Gould, "The Social Media Gospel,"in *Sharing God's News in New Ways,* 2nd ed. (Collegeville, MN: Liturgical Press, 2015), 9.

Stewardship is about being Christ in God's world for God's world. And now, in this century, we can, in the palm of our hand, use our phones to share the gospel throughout the world.

The Rev. Daniel Webster
Canon for Evangelism and Media, Episcopal Diocese of
Maryland

Five Talents—Fellowship of Ministry   SO 39

1 Kings 19:9–18

I alone am left. . . . (1 Kings 19:14)

In the rural mountains of Southeast Bolivia, pastors meet together each week to pray and save. Community savings provides a means for these church leaders to care for their families and to create a brighter future for their communities.

All pastors have difficulties that we have to face. Sometimes people forget that pastors are human who also feel, suffer, and have a family and needs. Our strength comes only from God, but every day there is something new to face and many times we don't have a Barnabas, Timothy, or Titus at our side.

I remember that the prophet Elijah was depressed when he was hiding in a mountain where God sent him. I was depressed because I also felt alone with all my problems. I was very sick—and I had many financial difficulties that my family was worried about. My church is small and it's in a rural area and other pastors almost never visit. But when [we started] the ministry of savings, it was nice to see all the pastors visit my church and pray for my family, my life, and the ministry.

The time of testimonies is very important for me because these testimonies help me grow spiritually and give me the strength to continue working. It's also very special because when someone shares his testimony, it opens his heart and we can express with freedom how we feel and so support one another. The savings ministry helped me spiritually because I have in the group a spiritual family that supports me. Church leaders often feel alone in ministry. Do you have a spiritual family that supports you? How are you partnering with other ministry leaders to give and invest in God's kingdom?

Pastor Hilarion Arenas
Tarija, Bolivia, with Five Talents USA

Five Talents—The Hand That Gives   SO 40

> When you give alms, do not let your left hand know what your right hand is doing, so that your alms may be done in secret; and your Father who sees in secret will reward you. (Matt. 6:3–4)

Jesus recognized giving as a central discipline of faith, one that is done without show or self-focus. The word for giving to the poor can be translated as "almsgiving," "giving to the needy," or "doing charity." As a Christian charity, Five Talents exists to help some of the world's poorest and most needy populations. The Episcopal Church is key in helping us mobilize givers as well as in coordinating ministry that truly helps and empowers the poor. Knowing God opens us up to a life of giving. May God bless each of us with the discipline of giving.

Rev. Jeff McKnight
Board Member, Five Talents USA

Five Talents—Interrupted by the Poor   SO 41

> "Tell me, what do you have in the house?" (2 Kings 4:2)

In the midst of his ministry to kings, Elisha stops to help an impoverished widow. The prophet's questions to the widow are striking. "What shall I do for you? Tell me, what do you have in the house?"

AND The widow answered, "Your servant has nothing in the house, except a jar of oil."

Elisha's encounter with the widow provides a biblical model for transformational ministry among the poor. Christian ministry gives voice to the marginalized and weak in their own homes. It recognizes and honors the dignity of the poor and helps them to use their God-given resources for good. This is the miracle of the oil. Have you ever taken stock of what is in your house? Are you willing to let the poor interrupt your ministry to kings?

Who knew that a few drops of oil could feed a family for months? Of course, it was important for the community to be involved. The widow expressed her faith by collecting and filling jars. Her neighbors each contributed an empty vessel. Through the widow's faith and work, her neighbors' concern, and God's provision, a business was born and a family saved. God's all-sufficient grace was poured into an area of neglect and need. It is my experience that God continues to fill empty vessels today.

Will Putz
Director of Development, Five Talents USA

Five Talents—It Is Enough   SO 42

There is a boy here who has five barley loaves and two fish. But what are they among so many people? (John 6:9)

Have you ever faced a daunting challenge and felt you had little to offer? In the hands of Jesus, it is enough. John's Gospel describes a little boy who surrenders his lunch to Jesus; the result is a miracle. In my work with Five Talents, I've been amazed how small investments surrendered to God can make a big impact. In South Sudan, for example, many young mothers have built sustainable businesses starting with less than two dollars. Your support of Five Talents is helping to change lives, offering hope, and creating opportunity in some of the most difficult places of our world.

One of the greatest rewards of wise stewardship is the prospect of multiplication. How could I not give, when God has given me so much? What is God calling you to surrender today?

Jim Oakes
CEO, Five Talents USA

Food Gathering   SO 43

In many of our congregations, we gather food for the hungry. Congregations are very good at asking. The pastor or a member of the congregation asks, and the people generously respond. Some of our congregations have their own food pantries; many others are part of an ecumenical community food bank or pantry hosted by volunteers. This is one way the Christian community can respond to local food insecurity. What we are not good about is thanking church members for their generous response.

————

Today we would like to thank all the members of our congregation who faithfully bring food to our church week by week to help feed those who are hungry in our community. Our thanks go as well to folks who make financial contributions. Our (church or community) food bank each week serves those most in need. You make a difference in providing much needed food, especially to families and our senior citizens. Thank you for your stewardship of sharing.

OR

Thank all of you who have responded to Jesus's call to feed the hungry. As part of our stewardship, we are responding out of our abundance to care for the neediest among us. When shopping, many of you buy a few items to bring to church on Sunday as part of your offering. Your response had been most heartening. We were able to give (name a quantity of food to the name the food bank) this past week. Through your generous gifts of both food and monetary gifts we are making a difference. On behalf of those who have been served we say, "Thank you."

Girl Scouts   SO 44

This Sunday we honor the Girl Scouts in our congregation on Girl Scout Sunday. Their oath is, "On my honor, I will try: To serve God and my country, To help people at all times, and To live by the Girl Scout Law." We give thanks for our congregation's generosity that enables Troop # to meet here each week. We are proud of all our Scouts and their faithful leaders. We all are well served when we follow their motto, "Be Prepared."

OR

We today recognize all the Girl Scouts in our congregation today, Girl Scout Sunday. I know many of us purchase their delicious cookies and financially support our Scouts. Our church has always been a supporter of scouting, and your generous giving, week by week, enables us to be a place where our scouts are spiritually strengthened to follow their motto, "Be Prepared."

Godly Play: Creation—Gifts So Big   SO 45
Genesis 1:1–2:3

What is the biggest gift you have ever received? *(Pause a few seconds.)* Some gifts are so big that we don't even notice them. They are hard to see. They are easy to take for granted. Sometimes we have to go back to the beginning, to a place of reflection, to even know the gift is there. In Godly Play, we celebrate the gifts of Creation in this way: these gifts are so big that we do not realize they are, in fact, gifts. We say, "In the beginning . . . In the beginning there was nothing." Think about that nothingness: cold, empty. And then God gave us the gifts of light and dark, water and firmament, land and sea, day and night, creatures that fly in the air and swim in the seas, creatures that walk on the earth, and the gift of a day to rest so that we can remember all our gifts. I wonder how the biggest gifts you have been given empower your own giving? Your gifts support our Godly Play program and empower our children with self-discovery and wondering skills. These skills are gifts—hard to see gifts—yet big gifts with which they can address life's challenges in an authentic relationship with their God. I wonder if you are aware of the lifelong gift you have given the children in our church through your pledge? Thank you.

W. Lee Dickson
Executive Director, Godly Play Foundation, Inc.

Godly Play—Great Pearl   SO 46

There was once someone who said such wonderful things and did such amazing things that people followed him. As they followed him, they heard him talking about a kingdom, but it was not the kingdom they lived in. It was not like any kingdom they had ever visited. It was not like any kingdom they had ever even heard of.

They couldn't help it. They had to ask him what the kingdom of heaven was like. One time when they asked him, he said:

> The kingdom of heaven is like when a person who buys and sells fine pearls, a merchant, goes in search for the great pearl. When he found the great pearl, he went and exchanged everything for the great pearl.[3]

As we follow Jesus, we can't help but wonder about what the kingdom of God is really like. We can't help but wonder about his parable of the merchant and the great pearl.

How did the merchant feel when everything was exchanged for the great pearl?

What exactly is the great pearl?

Where do you fit into this parable? How do you follow Jesus?

How does the parable of the great pearl affect your giving?

Thank you for your support of Godly Play—thank you for giving our children the gift of wonder.

The Rev. Regan M. Schutz
Director of Communications and Development, Godly Play
Foundation, Sewanee, Tennessee

---

3. Jerome W. Berryman, *The Complete Guide to Godly Play* (New York: Church Publishing, 2017), 3:99.

Godly Play—Parable of the Good Samaritan   SO 47

The parable of the good samaritan (Luke 10:30–35) is a complex parable. Someone is hurt and then given a gift of help. But when we hear this parable, we often overlook key points: there were bad men who robbed and beat a traveler, leaving him beside the road; priests and others walked by and left the man to die. Then the Samaritan comes. The people of the traveler did not like the people from Samaria. If fact, there was deep hatred and discrimination. But the person from Samaria does not pass by. He does not continue his journey. He stops and he helps. He gives the gift of aid, the gift of a beast to take the traveler to shelter, the gift of healing, the gift of money to allow his stay at the inn—time, talent, and treasure—and then he continues his journey. Let's look at it from the perspective of the wounded traveler. Did he like the person who gave him the gift of aid, of life, or did it make him angry, confused, and uncomfortable? In Godly Play we wonder which person was truly the neighbor. In times such as these—and perhaps in all times—we wonder, "Who is my neighbor?" We thank you for your support of our Godly Play program where we empower our children to engage in stories like this complex parable, to make meaning for themselves today, and to think about where they encounter the challenges of being a neighbor. Your pledge is a neighbor's gift to our children. Thank you.

W. Lee Dickson
Executive Director, Godly Play Foundation, Inc.

Godly Play—Ten Commandments   SO 48

In Godly Play, we tell our circles that "God gave the Ten Commandments to Moses. Moses gave them to the people, and they gave them to us." We know from the Bible that God first tried to give the Ten Commandments directly to the people, but they were not ready or able to accept them directly. The gift was too big; God's presence was too awesome. Sometimes it takes several sets of hands to bring us what we need. As stewards of the kingdom of God, we serve as Christ's hands in bringing God's gifts to fruition and to each other. Working in community is at the heart of this practice and at the heart of who we are as the body of Christ. We pass the plate from person to person because together we can do so much more than on our own—together we can serve God more fully.

Another thing we explain to our circles is "God did not say that these are the 'ten easy things to do.' They are the Ten Best Ways to Live—the Ten Commandments. They are hard, perhaps even impossible, but we are supposed to try." And so it is with stewardship, with our work in community. We may feel small and inadequate, the work may seem insurmountable, yet we must try. With each of us trying, we have a chance. We must stretch our giving of time and resources until we fear we might break because that is when we will begin to understand God's ultimate sacrifice. It may seem impossible, but every time we try, we get a little bit closer to the realm of God.

Thank you for bringing in the realm of God through your gifts of time and resources. Thank you for supporting Godly Play as we strive to model the Ten Best Ways to Live for all generations, and for the glory of God.

The Rev. Regan M. Schutz
Director of Communications and Development, Godly Play
Foundation, Sewanee, Tennessee

Gratitude for the Community of Faith   SO 49

Take a minute to ground yourself, close your eyes, and breathe deeply. Our lives are rushed and filled with worries about our church, our community, and the people we love. In the midst of the turmoil of life, take a moment to ground yourself. Remember that you are created in the image of God, remember that God has called you by name to do this work and has given you all you need to do it. We often need to be reminded that we have been called and that God has given us all we need. The community of faith is there to constantly remind us of this, especially when the path gets difficult or the trees are too thick to see the way. Allow your heart to fill with love and gratitude for your community of faith and for those who walk with you on the journey.

The Rev. Kristen Looney
Director of Partnerships, Religious Freedom Center of the
Newseum Institute, Washington, DC

Greeters   SO 50

Greeters are members of your congregation who are selected to welcome those who are your guests each Sunday as well as to welcome long-time members. I do not like the term "visitors." I don't have "visitors" come to my home, I have "guests." Those who come to your church on a Sunday morning need to be treated like guests in your home. There can be two to six greeters, depending on the size of your congregation. Some say we don't need greeters; we are a friendly congregation. What I have discovered is that the "friendlier" the congregation, the harder it is for a guest. I have found it effective for a greeter to stand next to the pastor as they shake hands after church. Then the greeter should take the guest to hospitality hour. The tendency at hospitality hour is for people to seek out their friends and inadvertently ignore the guest. A greeter has responsibility of introducing the guest to members after church. Some of the most effective greeters are those who have been members of your congregation for less than three years. They remember what it was like to be new.

This morning (or this week, if writing in the parish e-mail), as part of our stewardship, I want to thank those who welcome people before the service and act as greeters. You take on the responsibility of welcoming and introducing our guests to our church. We are growing because of your gracious hospitality in reaching out to those whom God has sent to us. You welcome all who worship with us, both newcomers and longtime parishioners. At hospitality hour you introduce them to our members and answer any questions they may have. It is because of your ministry that we are a welcoming church.

OR

Today we appreciate all who have said "yes" to being a greeter in our church. We are honoring you at our hospitality hour today. Your gracious hospitality in welcoming all who God sends to our church is making a difference as we strive to be Jesus Christ's face in our community. Your stewardship of time by being here and reaching out to greet all who enter here is much appreciated.

OR

This morning we give thanks for our greeters who Sunday by Sunday welcome all who enter our church. You are making a difference in the lives of those whom God is sending to us. Children, families, single and married adults are all welcome here in the name of the welcoming Christ. After church you also care for our guests and spend time with them at hospitality hour, introducing them to others and telling them about the ministries of our church. Your stewardship of time, presence, talent, and ability has reached out and made guests feel welcome. Your financial support of our church enables all of us to experience our vibrant worship of our Lord Jesus Christ.

Healing Brokenness   SO 51

Miriam was a leader even as a child. She navigated the survival of her baby brother Moses, helped lead the Hebrew people from oppression to freedom, and became a beloved prophet to her people. Strong, faithful, and resilient, she helped lead men, women, and children through the wilderness toward the Promised Land. Who are the women—the leaders, the prophets—in your faith community? Who are the women who have the courage to speak truth to power and fight for peace, justice, and equality in the face of resistance? Open your eyes just a little bit wider and see those in your midst who have already named the brokenness and have found a way to start healing it. Lift these women in your prayers and be grateful.

The Rev. Kristen Looney
Director of Partnerships, Religious Freedom Center of the
Newseum Institute, Washington, DC

Healing Service   SO 52

Many congregations have a midweek healing service, some with the laying on of hands and anointing. These services often are attended by a faithful few, and for some people, it is their most meaningful or only weekly worship. Everyone is always welcome. It is there for all who need God's healing, as well as providing an opportunity to offer healing prayers for members of the congregation and for loved ones.

Every week, we offer a weekday healing service with Eucharist at (time) on (day of the week). This service is also available to anyone who can't be here on Sunday to receive communion. Our worship focuses on the healing power of Jesus Christ. We offer anointing and the laying on of hands to people who seek healing. We also pray for all those on the parish prayer lists. This service, which includes a brief homily, is made possible through your faithful stewardship. Your giving enables Mother or Father _____ to be able be here to celebrate the Eucharist and preside at the service. Thank you for your faithful prayers and giving.

OR

Each week, we gather at (time) on (day of the week) to celebrate communion and have prayers of healing with anointing and the laying on of hands. A small but faithful group gathers to pray for those who have requested our prayers and for our congregation. We want to thank all who, through their generous giving, make it possible for us to offer this service to the members of our congregation. Your stewardship is making a difference in people's lives.

Homebound Communion   SO 53

Every Sunday, we gather to celebrate the Holy Eucharist and offer it to all who are present. Those who are unable to attend are our homebound parishioners. In the old days they were called "shut-ins," a name that came from a time before nursing homes and Alzheimer's centers. The elderly were literally shut in their bedrooms. Today we give thanks for our homebound parishioners, who are unable to be with us this morning. Each Sunday, we commission our Eucharistic Ministers to take the Eucharist to them in their home or facility that is caring for them.

Hospital Calls   SO 54

In your congregation the clergy make calls to parishioners in the hospital. For the clergy, this is a time of intimacy and connection. We pray together, often share communion, and the parish is present in spirit with us. That is made possible by its stewardship. This enables the pastor to have the time to make these calls in its name.

This past week I had the opportunity to be at (name of hospital) with (the person's name—if you have permission to share the name). We prayed together, and you all were there with us in spirit. I thank God for your faithful stewardship that enables me to be with our parishioners during a time of illness. Your generosity makes it possible for your clergy to be there. Thank you.

OR

This past week I visited (number of visits) members of our congregation (at name hospital or who are hospitalized). We prayed together and shared the communion. We spoke about last Sunday. You all were with us in spirit. I want to thank you for your faithful stewardship. Your offerings enable me to have the time to be there in the hospital. When you read or hear I have been in the hospital, please smile and feel good about that. Your stewardship made it possible.

Hospitality   SO 55

After Pentecost the women and men who believed in Jesus gathered to pray together, share the Lord's Supper, listen to the apostles' teaching, and share food and drink with each other. Jesus's actions showed us how important it is to share food and drink with others, especially with people we do not know. Every growing congregation knows how important this is. I am so glad we pattern ourselves after these early Christians. Our time of fellowship and hospitality after worship brings vitality to our congregation. Let us give thanks to those folks who prepare and serve the goodies and the beverages that make our time together so special. This time of hospitality provides a place to share our stories and open our lives to the blessing and surprises of God's Holy Spirit. The generosity of those who sign up for this ministry enriches the hospitality of our church. Thank you.

The Rev. Dr. Daniel L. Ogden
Retired Pastor, Reformed Church in America

Latino Ministry—Nuestros Comienzos   SO 56

Con el apoyo del personal de la oficina diocesana iniciamos nuestro ministerio latino en la iglesia de la Resurrección. Después de tocar muchas puertas y entregar panfletos en nuestro vecindario, comenzaron a llegar tres familias. Algunas buscando comida o un lugar caliente durante el invierno

Nuestro primer servicio eucarístico conto con ocho personas, tres niños y cinco adultos, incluida la sacerdote. Nos reuníamos alrededor del altar, para sentirnos acompañados y orar en círculo pidiendo por nuestras necesidades y las de los demás. Especialmente orábamos, por los que venían buscando entrar al país por la frontera con México. Esto nos fortalecía y mantenía unidos en un mismo sentir. Y así fuimos creciendo. La hora del café se convirtió en la obra social de la iglesia. Preparamos comida fuerte, arroz frijoles, tortillas etc. Además durante el momento de hospitalidad compartimos nuestras historias, de donde y por qué venimos. Esto nos ayudó a crecer como familia y darnos sostén los unos con los otros.

Lo maravilloso de todo esto es que cada uno de nosotros, trae de lo que tiene. Ya sean materiales de limpieza o para cocinar. Dejamos el dinero de las ofrendas, para pagar los gastos de gas, luz , agua etc. de la iglesia. El voluntariado para limpiar, reparar y pintar, ha crecido maravillosamente y hoy nuestra iglesia luce hermosa y digna para el Señor.

Nuestro ministerio sigue creciendo, pues hoy no solo damos comida caliente sino que proveemos un lugar donde informarse sobre el proceso de emigración en el país. Sin olvidar que el acompañamiento físico es lo fundamental en estos procesos.

El ministerio Latino en nuestra diócesis, es una obra de amor de los unos por los otros. Busca darle sentido a nuestra responsabilidad cristiana de cumplir uno de los mandamientos principales que nuestro Señor Jesucristo nos dejó: "Ama a tu prójimo como a ti mismo" (Mc.12:31, DHH).

Demos gracias a todos y todas en nuestra Diocesis de Maryland que mediante su mayordomía y apoyo financiero a su parroquia y luego el apoyo parroquial a la Diocese hacen este ministerio latino posible.

Revda. Margarita Santana

Latino Ministry—Our Beginnings

With support from the Diocese Office we initiated our Latino ministry at the Church of the Resurrection. After knocking on many doors and handing out leaflets in our community, three families began to arrive. Some searching for food or a warm place to be during the winter.

Eight people, three children and five adults including the priest, came to our first Eucharist service. We all gathered around the altar to feel companionship and pray in a circle, asking for our needs and those of others. We prayed especially for those who came into the country through the Mexican border. This strengthened us and united us in a shared sentiment. And thus we began to grow.

The coffee hour became the church's social workplace. We prepared hearty meals, rice, beans, tortillas, etc. In addition, during hospitality period we shared our stories, where we came from and why. This helped us grow as a family and helped us support one another.

The marvelous thing about this is that each one of us brings whatever he or she has, be it cleaning supplies or cooking materials. We left the offering money to pay for gas, electricity, water, and other church expenses. Volunteers to clean, repair, and paint have increased wonderfully and today our church looks beautiful and worthy of the Lord.

Our ministry continues to grow and today we not only offer hot meals, but also provide a place for getting information about the process of immigration to the country, never forgetting that physical accompaniment is fundamental in these processes.

The Latino ministry in our diocese is a labor of love for each other and by each other. It seeks to infuse the Christian sense of responsibility to follow one of the main commandments our Lord Jesus Christ left us: "You shall love your neighbor as yourself" (Mark 12:31).

Our thanks to all in our diocese who through their giving to their parish, and then their congregation's giving to our diocese that makes this ministry possible.

Rev. Margarita Santana
Canon for Latino Ministry, Episcopal Diocese of Maryland
Translated by Pura Reyes Gilestra and Reparto Landrau

Latino Ministry—Ganar o Perder   SO 57

Jesús dijo: "El que halla su vida, la perderá; y el que pierde su vida por causa de mí, la hallará." (Mt. 10:39)

Cuando era niña no participaba en muchas competencias por temor a perder.

Aunque muchos afirmar que el participar en sí, ya es una ganancia, no estaba segura de ello.

Toda nuestra vida se trata de ganar o perder. Pero, para ganar o perder necesitamos un elemento importante que es el de arriesgarse. Hay un dicho que dice: "El que no se arriesga ni gana ni pierde".

Como cristianos sentimos miedo de "perder" amistades por declarar públicamente a que denominación pertenecemos. Incluso parientes cercanos se nos alejan por declarar nuestra preferencia sexual o simpatía política.

Lo mismo sucede cuando sentimos que ofrendamos más de lo que acostumbramos. Sentimos temor de que nuestro presupuesto personal quede deficitario. Oh, sí participamos demasiado en cosas de la iglesia, ya no tendremos tiempo para nuestros asuntos personales.

Cuando sentimos temor al arriesgarnos, generalmente ponemos más atención en las pérdidas que en las ganancias.

Parafraseando el evangelio de Mateo en su capítulo 10 verso 29, nos dice: "si perdemos la vida por causa de Cristo, será ganancia".

Me gusta usar la palabra invertir, mejor que "dar". Pues todo lo que doy, se me traduce en ganancia. Tiempo, talento y tesoro, cuando los invierto gano el doble, quizás el triple.

Cuando aprendí esto deje de tener miedo a participar en competencias. Pues comprendí que el mismo hecho de participar ya es ganancia.

Algo que me ayudo fue poner mi fe en que tendría ganancia, como seguro de mi inversión. Hoy puedes hacer tu lo mismo, pues "lo poco en nuestras manos es mucho en la manos de Dios".

Gracias a todos y todas que invierten sus recursos financieros en proveer para esta comunidad de fe.

Revda. Margarita Santana

Latino Ministry—Winning and Losing

Jesus said: "Those who find their life will lose it, and those who lose their life for my sake will find it." (Matt. 10:39)

When I was a child I did not participate much in competitions for fear of losing. Although many say that participation in itself is a win, I was not sure of that.

Our whole lives are about winning or losing. But in order to win or to lose, we need an important element, which is taking a risk. There is a saying that says: "If you do not try, you neither win nor lose."

As Christians we fear "losing" friends by publicly stating what denomination we belong to. Even close relatives will distance themselves from us because we state our sexual preference or our political views.

This also happens when we feel we have given more than what we usually do. We fear that our personal budget may be negatively affected. Or if we participate too much in church activities, we will not have time for our personal matters.

When we are afraid to take risks, we usually pay more attention to the losses rather than the wins.

Paraphrasing Mathew's Gospel in chapter 10, verse 29 he says: "If we lose our life for Christ, it is a win."

I like to use the word "invest" instead of "give." Because everything I give translates into a gain. When I invest time, talent, and treasure, I win back double, maybe even triple.

When I learned this, I stopped being afraid of participating in competitions because I understood that participation itself was already a win.

Something that helped me was putting my faith in that I would have a win, in order to ensure my investment. Today you can do the same because "what little we have in our hands is a lot in the hands of God."

Thanks to all who invest their money in providing this community of faith.

Rev. Margarita Santana
Canon for Latino Ministry, Episcopal Diocese of Maryland
Translated by Pura Reyes Gilestra and Reparto Landrau

Legacy Society—Diocese   SO 58

I believe every diocese large or small should have a diocesan legacy society. After many years of hard work, we have one in the Diocese of Maryland: All Saints Legacy Society. It consists of four hundred and eight-three households from fifty-four congregations. It includes forty-three clergy households. We list all the members by congregation in our annual diocesan convention booklet. Some congregations have twenty-nine households who are members, and some have just one. The bishop invites each household to an annual recognition service at our cathedral, followed by a reception at the bishop's official residence. The invitations are hand addressed. In this way we thank those who have remembered their church, the diocese, or the diocesan conference center in their will/estate plans.

This Sunday (date) at (time) our diocese will be hosting the Annual Recognition Service at our cathedral for the members of the diocesan All Saints Legacy Society. We have (number) households who have remembered our church in their will/estate plans and are part of the All Saints Legacy Society. We thank all who are members of our parish's legacy society. By including us in your estate plans, you have made us a member of your family.

OR

On Sunday (date) the Diocese of _____ will recognize all the households who have remembered their parish, the diocese, or the diocesan conference center in their will/estate plans. At St. _____ we have (number) members of our parish's (or congregation's) legacy society. By joining the local parish's legacy society, one also becomes a member of our diocesan (proper name) legacy society. We thank all who are members, because they included this parish, the diocese, or the diocesan conference center in their will/estate plans.

Legacy Society—Parish   SO 59

I believe every congregation should have a legacy society. It can be named after a prominent date, such as the year your parish was founded, or the

(Name of Parish) All Saints Legacy Society. Your vestry can choose the name and then invite members of your congregation to join by remembering the congregation in their will/estate plans. The society can have a few members or many. Every pledge card should have this check-off box: "[ ] I have remembered our church in my will/estate plans." In January, the pastor and the chair of the Planned Giving or Stewardship Committee need to write a letter to the person inviting them to become a member of the parish's legacy society.

On appropriate Sundays, the rector of an Episcopal church should remind the congregation of these words from the Book of Common Prayer.

The Minister of the Congregation is directed to instruct the people, from time to time, about the duty of Christian parents to make prudent provision for the well-being of the families, and of all persons to make wills, while they are in health, arranging for the disposal of their temporal goods, not neglecting, if they are able, to leave bequests for religious and charitable uses. (BCP, 445)

Then the rector would add, "This morning we are honoring and thanking those parishioners, our saints, who have remembered our church in their will/estate plans and have joined our legacy society. We have listed their names on the back of our bulletin today. A special cake at the hospitality hour is given in appreciation of their commitment.

National Preparedness Month   SO 60

Then I heard the voice of the Lord saying, "Whom shall I send, and who will go for us?" And I said, "Here am I; send me!" (Isa. 6:8)

Are we ready to respond to God's call to be sent out to do the work of God? How do we prepare to be sent? To me one of the most important parts of the liturgy is the dismissal: "Go in peace to love and serve the Lord." Serve God by serving others. Serve family, neighbors, and community. Serve those close and far off. Serve those we know and those we don't. Strive to live out the whole of our baptismal covenant.

An important part of being sent out to do the work of God is being prepared. Former President Barack Obama declared September National Preparedness Month "to encourage all Americans to recognize the importance of preparedness and work together to enhance our resilience and readiness." At Episcopal Relief and Development, one way we love and serve the Lord is by working with the church, at home and abroad, to empower communities to thoughtfully prepare for both natural and human-made disasters. We work with our partners to help deliver necessities of life—food, water, shelter, and friendship. We also stay in relationship with impacted communities long after the crisis is over to help heal, recover, and rebuild.

What is God asking us to do today? How can we prepare for tomorrow? How do we steward our assets to help those in need? As we plan and prepare for inevitable disasters in our own communities, we need to pray for those around the world who will be impacted by circumstances beyond their control—hurricanes, earthquakes, mudslides, droughts, wars—how can we support them in their hour of need?

Episcopal Relief and Development gives thanks for all the people of the Episcopal Church who help us serve others.

Robert W. Radtke
President, Episcopal Relief and Development,
New York, New York

Not Out of Duty: A Dog's Death   SO 61

From Psalm 9: "I will give thanks to the LORD with my whole heart . . ."

Kiril died today. His last labored breath, as if it were my own, misted across the vet's linoleum floor. We chanted to him "Anima Christi," which I had heard at the Benedictine Monastery in Bombay, India. And we wept. The night vigils, special diets, routines of shots and pills, baths and clean-ups ended. A love rhythm had attended our great, white Samoyed, "the Christmas dog" descended from Artic wolves, a reindeer herder adored by Eskimos and Russian czars. God said we have dominion over them (Gen. 1), but Kiril's unbeguiled love and loyalty ruled us. His deep brown eyes coaxed us to understand that giving is granting others the essence of our being—as Christ loved us and gave himself for us. Giving is grace to the giver. Kiril's heart drank life. His body instinctively gave it to others. Grace begetting gratitude.

When, however, giving is reduced to duty, it is hollow. Cleaning dirty linens and soiled tarps, packing up medicines, syringes, insulin, and bowls for the animal shelter was perfunctory, like signing a check or clicking an e-account to the church for her "services." These are outward signs of inward shallows. True stewardship is pledging the heart in the realm of the peaceable kingdom (Isa. 11). Then corporate giving becomes corporeal, the manifestation of God's grace working in us for others. Therein lies joy. Witness the animals!

The Rev. Jane R. Bearden, STM, Hon rt.
The Presbytery of Baltimore, Maryland

Our Island Home   SO 62

At your command all things came to be: the vast expanse of interstellar
space, galaxies, suns, the planets in their courses, and this fragile earth,
our island home. (Eucharistic Prayer C, BCP, 370)

It seems that our Creator is amazingly expansive, creating a universe with a vastness beyond real human comprehension but within our capacity for appreciation. It also appears that by creating human beings that our Lord was enlisting partners in creation, beings that the Holy Spirit would love and call into action. The Spirit nudges us from within and without and has given us the capacity and freedom to create or destroy, and is confident that we will choose to live responsibly, using the beauty and order of God's own creation as our model. We are now in the midst of a living experience that requires God-like spirituality, God-like love for others, God-like responsibility. We are earth's stewards, God's stewards in this place. As we consider how we can help individually and as a community, may we give with thanksgiving and with confidence that we are the Lord's ambassadors and stewards for the future of our island home.

The Rev. Stephen Parker
Author, *Bridges: Embracing Faith and Science*, retired
Chaplain, Salisbury School, Salisbury, Connecticut

Overseas Ministries Study Center—A Dramatic Reversal   SO 63

> For as in one body we have many members, and not all the members have the same function, so we, who are many, are one body in Christ, and individually we are members one of another. We have gifts that differ according to the grace given to us. (Rom. 12:4–6)

Today's communication and transportation technologies link us more immediately and closely than ever before. But "being linked" is not the same as "being one." Accenting Christian diversity and oneness, the apostle Paul depicted our unity in Christ in a way that sounds contemporary, especially given the dramatic demographic transformation of Christianity in the world.

In 1900, there were five times as many Christians in Europe, Russia, and North America than in Africa, Asia, Latin America, and Oceania. Today, the situation is reversed. This reversal occurred both because of and in spite of the modern missionary movement. Musing on what this might mean today, historian of mission Andrew Walls says, "We now live at a time when the Church is multicultural. I think that the fullness of the stature of Christ will emerge only when Christians from all these cultures come together."[4]

---

4. "The Expansion of Christianity: An Interview with Andrew Walls," *Christian Century* 117, no. 22 (August 2–9, 2000): 795.

Since 1922, the Overseas Ministries Study Center (OMSC) in New Haven, Connecticut, has hosted more than 25,000 missionaries, church leaders, and scholars from almost 100 countries and all church traditions. OMSC *engages in mission with the world Christian movement* through our residential community, study program, and academic journal (*International Bulletin of Mission Research*). Part of our mission is to encourage churches today to rethink what it means to be "one body in Christ, and . . . members one of another." We are grateful for the generous support of so many people.

Rev. Dr. Thomas John Hastings
Executive Director, Overseas Ministries Study Center,
New Haven, Connecticut

Overseas Ministries Study Center—Putting God's Love into Practice   SO 64

Bear one another's burdens, and in this way you will fulfill the law of Christ. (Gal. 6:2)

Each year on April 23, the Episcopal Calendar of the Church Year honors "Toyohiko Kagawa (1888–1960), Renewer of Society," on the anniversary of his death. Kagawa dared to believe that the Holy Spirit enables us to put the "redemptive love of Jesus Christ" into practice. To Kagawa, "redemptive love" meant, "You mess up, I clean up your mess and refuse to assign any blame."

Led to faith as a teenager by American missionaries, Kagawa was one of the best-known Japanese evangelists and social reformers of the twentieth century. Taking seriously the call to take the gospel across social and cultural boundaries, Kagawa left his seminary dormitory in 1909 to live in Kobe's worst slum, where he lived and worked with his wife, Haru, for more than ten years.

Friend and advocate of children, women, and the poor, best-selling novelist and poet, religious educator, labor and union organizer, cooperative movement leader, interdisciplinary thinker, economic theorist, advocate for racial justice, peacemaker, apologetic theologian, and prophetic provocateur, Toyohiko—always with Haru's collaboration and support—was founder of several still-thriving consumer, educational, medical, financial, labor, and agricultural cooperatives, two-time nominee for the Nobel Prize in Literature, and four-time nominee for the Nobel Peace Prize. Think of other great spiritual leaders of the twentieth century—Mahatma Gandhi, Albert Schweitzer, Martin Luther King Jr., Mother Teresa—and you will have a sense of the stature this couple achieved during their lifetimes, as well as their lasting legacy.

We give thanks for spiritual pioneers like the Kagawas, who stewarded their resources to enrich the lives of those in need.

Rev. Dr. Thomas John Hastings
Executive Director, Overseas Ministries Study Center,
New Haven, Connecticut

Providing Sanctuary   SO 65

We call a place a sanctuary to mean both a place we can worship God and a place where we feel safe from danger. This church provides sanctuary where people can come to tune out the noise of the world, to pray, and to seek God.

People who feel troubled or afraid or who need help often seek out the church. Because we are a caring, generous congregation, we welcome everyone regardless of who they are. In this sanctuary, people in need can find someone who cares and who will offer encouragement for their difficult journey. We as a church exist to provide sanctuary as often as it is needed. Thank you.

The Rev. Dr. Daniel L. Ogden
Retired Pastor, Reformed Church in America

Religious Freedom   SO 66

Every Sunday, I walk into my church without worrying whether someone will violently attack me because I am a Christian. I can wear a cross,
I can wear my clergy collar, I can walk through the doors without wondering whether a mob of protesters will be there taunting me or calling
me to leave the country, to go home. I don't have to worry that graffiti
will cover the walls of my church or that bricks will be thrown through
the stained glassed windows. As a Christian, I have privilege living in
America that many of my Muslim, Jewish, Hindu, and Sikh brothers
and sisters don't have. I experience religious freedom. I know that this
privilege comes with tremendous responsibility—the responsibility to
protect this right for every American of all religions and none. Let us recognize and be grateful for this freedom and commit ourselves to ensur-
ing all people experience this freedom.

The Rev. Kristen Looney
Director of Partnerships, Religious Freedom Center of the
Newseum Institute, Washington, DC

Sabbatical   SO 67

I want to thank all of you for my sabbatical. It is truly a gift, after serving
you for these past _____ years as your pastor. It will be a time of renewal
and reflection for me. I plan to _____, and I know you
will be with me in spirit and in prayer. I believe it is an investment in
our future ministry together. Your financial support of this sabbatical
reflects your faithful stewardship in time, abilities, and money. Again,
thank you.

OR

I will be leaving for my sabbatical on _____. I want to
share my appreciation to our vestry and to you the congregation for
granting me these _____ months for a time of refreshment and spiritual
reflection. I plan to _____. It is truly a gift that I will always

appreciate, an investment in our time together as we strive to love and serve our Lord Jesus Christ. Thank you, thank you, thank you!

Seminary—Theological Education (January 25)   SO 68

Today we remember (seminary / divinity school) in our prayers as we remember Paul, the patron saint of our theological education. Our seminaries prepare men and women to serve as clergy in our Episcopal Church (your denomination). Each year our congregation sends $_____ to support (name of seminary). This gift comes from your generous offerings. Thank you for showing your appreciation of our clergy. We pray God will continue to call men and women to serve in Christ's church as God called Paul.

OR

Our church gives $_____ to support (name of seminary or divinity school). We ask your prayers today for (name of seminary) that it may continue to prepare fine men and women to serve as deacons and priests in our church. We do this on the Sunday closest to January 25th, St. Paul's Day. As God called Paul to preach the gospel, we pray God will continue to call men and women to serve in God's church. Thank you, thank you, thank you for your generous giving.

St. Nicholas of Myra at Christmastide   SO 69

The Bishop of Myra in Asia Minor named Nicholas became well known throughout the world for his generosity and compassion. There are no written records about him from his time as bishop, but legends abound. The legends come from many cultures about this man's miraculous power and his abundance in giving. In some of these legends he encouraged others to give generously as well. As you may know, he was the inspiration for the stories of Santa Claus, or St. Nick, who brings gifts to children on Christmas Eve. During this time of frenzied holiday shopping when we fret about selecting just the right gift for a special person, let us remember the folks whom Bishop Nicholas cared for: people, especially children, in need. Let our gifts this season to people who need our support follow Bishop Nicholas's example of generosity. Please give generously.

The Rev. Elizabeth Rust Masterson
Rector (retired), St. Nicholas' Church, Newark, Delaware

Twitter   SO 70

"Stewardship is giving with no strings attached. It is related to creation and my place in it." So wrote the Rev. Dan Matthews, former rector, Trinity, Wall Street, in an article in the winter 2003 edition of the *Trinity News*, "The Ways We Give."

Every day, millions of people share new chapters of their stories on social media. We're always talking about our place in creation to dozens if not hundreds of followers on Facebook, Twitter, and Instagram. Why not use our newsfeeds and Twitter streams to tell the world about the gifts God gives us and how we, in turn, give to others?

The Gospel of Matthew (5:14–16) tells us we "are the light of the world." And no one hides a lamp but puts on the lamp stand for all to see. We now have the opportunity and the means to let our light shine that Dan Matthews didn't when he wrote his article. But we can now tell our stories of the joy of giving with no strings attached that is the same way God gives to us. We don't have to earn our next breath, or that beautiful sunrise, or the life-giving rain. God's gift is freely given. Stewardship is giving the way God gives: unconditionally, expecting nothing in return.

The Rev. Canon Daniel Webster
Canon for Evangelism and Media, Episcopal Diocese of
Maryland

Ushers   SO 71

Ushers are some of the unsung heroes in our congregations. Sunday by Sunday they arrive early, hold the programs, and give them to all whom Jesus brings to worship. They have a welcoming smile, warmly greet the longtime members as well as Sunday guests (newcomers). They gather the offering. In many congregations, they assist with guiding parishioners to communion.

––––––

This morning, we give thanks for our ushers. They greet us every Sunday morning with a smile, whether we are longtime members or guests here for the first time. They have a number of duties: they pass out the service leaflets (programs, bulletins), they gather our offering and bring it forward to be blessed, they are available to answer any questions, and they guide us to communion. They will offer assistance with any emergencies. We thank all who practice their ministry of usher.

OR

This week we honor our guild of ushers. Our ushers warmly greet us every Sunday with a smile, whether we are longtime members or guests here for the first time. They hand out bulletins (leaflets, programs) not only to help us follow the service and but also to read about the exciting miniseries taking place in our congregation. They gather our Sunday offering, given to support our ministries. Then they present at the altar the money that we are offering for God's work. We say "thank you" to each of them, "Thank you, thank you, thank you."

Vestry   SO 72

The vestry is the governing body for the congregation in the Episcopal Church. Vestry members usually are elected by the congregation for a three-year term. In many congregations this election is competitive. In other congregations a nominating committee offers the number of candidates to fill the vacant positions. Vestry members should be pledgers in the congregation. How can they spend other parishioners' money if they themselves are not financially committed to the congregation's mission and ministries?

––––––––––––

We will be electing new members to our vestry at our annual meeting (time, day, and date). I want to thank all those who have chosen to stand for election. They are leaders in our congregation. They all are living out their stewardship by giving of their time, their talents and abilities, and their money to support the mission and ministries of our church.

OR

Today we are electing our vestry members. I want to thank each of them for saying yes to being leaders and decision makers in our church. Our vestry members faithfully worship on Sunday, meet monthly, (serve on committees,) and pledge for the support of our ministries. They are living out their stewardship. I want to thank all of you who give to support our beloved church.

Veterans Day—We Are
the Stewards of Everything   SO 73

Then God said, "Let us make humankind in our image, in our likeness, and let them be stewards over the fish of the sea and the birds of the air, over the livestock, over all the earth, and over all the creatures that move along the ground." In fact, over everything! (Gen. 1:26–28, paraphrase)

We Christians have grown accustomed to hearing preachers tell us that God gave us "dominion" over all of his creation. But I sometimes wonder if we take God seriously. As a bishop and shepherd to military and federal chaplains and their families, I see them not only as ordained servants but also as stewards of our great nation. Service members in the Army, Navy, Air Force, Marine Corps, and Coast Guard all protect the freedoms we cherish. What are those freedoms? Well, there are the freedoms so nobly expressed by President James Madison in the first ten amendments to the U.S. Constitution, what we call "The Bill of Rights." Then there are the freedoms President Franklin Delano Roosevelt declared in a major speech during the Great Depression, later immortalized by Norman Rockwell in his "Four Freedoms" paintings: Freedom from Want, Freedom of Speech, Freedom to Worship, and Freedom from Fear. All of these freedoms are encapsulated in the 1948 United Nations Declaration of Human Rights. But what about those freedoms we take for granted or treat as if they are rights: home ownership, jobs, health care, public education, and transportation? Only in America are these blessings all but guaranteed.

We live in an age of "entitlement," as it's called. We go about our daily routines in a free and open society, never stopping to think how our lifestyles are secured. Just as the blessed Apostle Paul reminds us that we are not our own, but "were bought with a price," in reference to the sacrifice of Jesus on the cross (1 Cor. 6:20), so it is that our freedoms as citizens were purchased with the lives of patriots and the blood of warriors who willingly gave up the amenities we enjoy. For this we should be grateful.

With the freedoms come responsibilities. When Adam and Eve were in the garden, their "original sin" came in the form of their choosing willfulness over obedience. They quickly forgot God's instructions and began to behave as freedom meant license. However, true freedom is God's service (BCP, 99). True freedom comes from obedience to the God who makes us stewards over everything, not that we should be dictators or abusers, but servants.

The Rt. Rev. Carl Walter Wright
VII Bishop Suffragan for the Armed Forces and Federal
Ministries

Weddings   SO 74

Last Saturday, we celebrated a wonderful wedding here at our church. The sanctuary was full, and it was a joyous service as the couple committed themselves to each other in the eyes of God. We all witnessed their commitment and were moved by their love for each other. I want to thank all of you for your generous giving that enables us to offer a beautiful church, clergy to officiate, and place for family and friends to gather to bless and support a marriage. Whenever you hear or read about a marriage taking place here, smile; you helped make it happen.

Wills/Estate Plans   SO 75

The Book of Common Prayer states:

> The Minister of the Congregation is directed to instruct the people, from time to time, about the duty of Christian parents to make prudent provision for the well-being of the families, and of all persons to make wills, while they are in health, arranging for the disposal of their temporal goods, not neglecting, if they are able, to leave bequests for religious and charitable uses. (BCP, 445)

This morning I have read, as instructed in our Book of Common Prayer, the direction that we all need to have an up-to-date will. None of us want to "leave a mess" for our family when we enter eternal life. Remember we have a 100 percent mortality rate here. The prayer book also encourages us to remember our congregation in our will/estate plans. For those who have done so, I say, "Thank you." For those who are considering doing so, I encourage you to do it now.

OR

Our e-mail blast this week included the following quote from our Book of Common Prayer (include the quote above).

Our prayer book calls on each of us to have an up-to-date will/estate plan for our family and to include, if possible, a bequest to our church. Your bequest will strengthen our church for the future. Remember the state of (name of state where the church is located) has a "will" for every member of our congregation. The laws of the state direct how our estate will be distributed if we die without writing our own will. Each of us has the freedom to write our own will and share our estate in ways that benefit those whom we love, as well as those institutions that have nurtured us and enriched our lives, like our church.

Wondrous Creator   SO 76

Dear Lord, You are the wondrous Creator of things big and small. You are Lord of the macro and micro worlds that we perceive, and you are our Lord in immanent and transcendent ways. We celebrate the magnificence of your created order, especially our earthly home, a Goldilocks planet, not too big and not too small, not too hot and not too cold, not too easy for us and not too tough for us, where challenges continually exist and evolve from decade to decade, century to century, millennium to millennium, eon to eon.

We thank you for loving us enough to give us the responsibility of the stewardship of our earthly home where in partnership with you we may create the possibilities for goodness to abound. Giving of our means is one important way of doing that. Thank you for the privilege of being individual stewards as well as a community of stewards, having the vision of and faith in a brighter future in the company of people who can bring it about.

The Rev. Stephen Parker
Author, *Bridges: Embracing Faith and Science*, retired
Chaplain, Salisbury School, Salisbury, Connecticut

Youth   SO 77

Let know no one despise your youth, but set the believers an example in speech and conduct, in love, in faith, in purity. (1 Tim. 4:12)

As a minister to what everyone over thirty calls "the future of the church" or the "next generation," I often have to remind adults that the young people are here now. They have a longing for God, for service, and for a bond with their community. Often these needs are met more conveniently by school friends, a part-time job, or hours on the computer. All these activities are an attempt to fill a hole in their soul.

These young people are ready to be called to serve a greater purpose than themselves. This piece of scripture is our diocesan youth motto. It reminds our young people that they are called from birth to build the kingdom of God on earth. A huge part of our diocesan ministry is peer ministry. We lift up the young people around the diocese into roles of leadership with one another. Our youth direct their own retreats, have voice and vote at diocesan convention, and their actions change the world around them through mission. All they need is some encouragement to seek their soul's desire in serving God's higher purpose, and the often more complicated process of creating a worldwide community of unconditional love. I want to thank all who support ministry to youth in your parish or in our diocese.

God, you have called all your children by name, regardless of age. Let us come to you, before all others, when our souls feel empty or our hearts ache. Give us grace and courage to proclaim your holy presence in our lives through our own styles. May service to your people give our souls strength to help build your kingdom here on earth. Amen.

Thank you to all of you who support our youth ministry in our congregation and diocese.

Kate Riley
Diocesan Youth Missioner, The Episcopal Diocese of
Maryland

Youth Choir   SO 78

"Let the little children come to me, and do not stop them; for it is such as these that the kingdom of heaven belongs." (Matt. 19:14)

The voices of children cannot help but lift the hearts of anyone who hears them. Their sounds at play and their laughter delight us. But their combined voices in song touch us deeply. Without a director to teach them or sheet music to read, they would not be here to sing for you today. At choir practice, they are learning to understand music, to appreciate this great gift and to join their voices together to offer praise and thanksgiving. It is often an experience that will affect their whole lives. Thank you for supporting our children's choir by your pledge.

Constance Hegarty
Retired Organist and Choir Director,
Windsor Locks, Connecticut

Section VII

Planned Giving Meditations

There are ten meditations concerning planned giving in the planned giving sections:

* Legacy Society—Parish
* Legacy Society—Diocese
* Wills and Bequest

Each of these can be adapted to your congregation and made relevant for your members.

James Murphy and Kenneth Quigley, both of the Episcopal Church Foundation, wrote nine meditations. The Rev. Melvin Amerson of the Methodist Foundation (Austin, Texas) wrote the tenth meditation. The meditations can be published in your Sunday bulletin program, monthly newsletter, and weekly parish e-mail. Over the course of time they will help educate your congregation on planned giving.

Either You Write a Will or the State Will   PG 1

Most people prefer not talking about death. Consequently, most people die without a written will. So what happens then? If you don't have a will, the state has already written one for you. And guess how the state will distribute your assets after you die? Lawyers are first in line, of course. Then taxes, creditors, and finally loved ones. Nothing goes to charity.

Also, your survivors get to pay the maximum in estate and inheritance taxes. With a will, you control applicable taxes, and you determine what charities you want to be part of your legacy. You release your family from unnecessary turmoil and delay in settling your estate.

If you don't have a will, make one. If you haven't looked at your will in a while, check it out. Even the Book of Common Prayer has something to say about wills. On page 445 it reads:

> The Minister of the Congregation is directed to instruct the people, from time to time, about the duty of Christian parents to make prudent provision for the well-being of their families, and of all persons to make wills while they are in health, arranging for the disposal of their temporal goods, not neglecting, if they are able, to leave bequests for religious and charitable uses.

Which in a bizarre way reminds me of a joke. A grandfather was sitting on the porch after dinner with his three young grandsons. The older boy asks the grandfather to make the croaking noise that frogs make. "No, not tonight," he replied. "I'm not feeling that well." The second grandson continues:

"Please, grandpa, you know the noise we mean. We want to hear the frog croak."

"Not tonight," grandpa responded, getting a little annoyed. "Why do you insist on my making the frog noise?"

The smallest grandson pipes up. "Well, mommy says that when grandpa croaks, we all get to go to Disneyworld."

Kenneth H. Quigley
Senior Program Director, Endowment Management
Solutions, Episcopal Church Foundation

Endowing My Pledge   PG 2

I remember a gentleman approaching eighty at a midwestern parish telling me about his many years spent worshiping in his church and the difference it had made in his life. He also asked me if he should endow his pledge, a question I have often been asked by concerned parishioners. Many worry that as demographic changes reduce church membership, the parishes they helped sustain for decades will suffer without sufficient financial support. Although there are some risks when parishes grow too dependent on endowment income, most of the time such a gift can be a wonderful testimony. After accounting for other commitments, those with the capacity and motivation may wish to make this decision.

As I suggested to my octogenarian inquirer, if you are considering this, review your maximum annual pledge during your lifetime, then multiply that by twenty-five to come up with a value to leave as an endowment that would produce income equal to your pledge—essentially, a 3 to 4 percent draw to the parish in perpetuity, while allowing for growth to keep up with inflation. If this is something you are able to do, be cautious not to restrict your gift's income to a purpose; simply allow it be used as needed for parish operating income, simulating your annual pledge. I believe that gentleman chose to make such a bequest in his will.

Even if you are not in a position to leave such a large gift, if you are committed to the future mission of your congregation you could leave a percentage of your estate or the remainder value of an IRA or some other gift. Regardless of the eventual value, your planned gift can still be your commitment to an uncertain future and enable your parish to be transformational for others for many generations to come.

James W. N. Murphy, CFRE
Managing Program Director, Financial Resources,
Episcopal Church Foundation

The Essence of Planned Giving   PG 3

In a way, planned giving can be summarized in the phrase "they trusted where they could not see"—a line from the Wheaton College hymn. And the next verse (imagine these lines in the context of a church community):

> A hundred years pass like a dream,
> Yet early founders still are we,

Whose works are greater than they seem,
Because of what we yet shall be
In the bright noon of other days,
Mid other souls and other ways.[1]

Or from Maya Angelou: "When we cast our bread upon the waters, we can presume that someone downstream whose face we will never know will benefit from our action, as we who are downstream from another, will profit from the grantor's gift."[2]

Or from Henry Ward Beecher: "We should so live and labor in our times that what came to us as a seed may go to the next generation as blossom, and what came to us as a blossom may go to them as fruit."[3]

These quotes express a basic concept of our life together in community, our reliance on the generosity of others, and our duty to future generations. In essence we own nothing. We are stewards of God's bounty. Caretakers. For a brief period we are given time, energy, and resources. What we choose to do with these gifts ultimately defines the character of our life and the depth of our spiritual understanding.

Endowments embody this concept. Endowments reflect the generosity of prior generations. They challenge the skill of the current generation to manage those funds responsibly and to use them wisely. And they invite the congregation to develop and sustain a vision for the future.

Kenneth H. Quigley
Senior Program Director, Endowment Management
Solutions, Episcopal Church Foundation

Faith vs. Fear   PG 4

A few years ago I met with a church in the Southeast. They had an $8 million endowment and were spending nothing from it. When I asked

---

1. Used with permission: Wheaton College Office of Legal Affairs & Risk Management.
2. http://izquotes.com/quote/387865.
3. http://www.giga-usa.com/quotes/authors/henry_ward_beecher_a016.htm

why, they said one never knew when it might be needed—there could be a hurricane, for example, and they might need to rebuild the church. The Bible tells us not to worry about tomorrow. God will provide, it teaches. It doesn't argue against possessions, but rather against possessiveness. When we act out of fear—a desire to grasp, to hold onto rather than share what we have—we diminish the power of our God. If we have faith the size of a mustard seed, Jesus said, it is enough to move mountains. By hoarding possessions to guard against a possible catastrophe, we miss the abundance of God's blessings. Remember the parable of the talents.

> Give and it will be given to you. A good measure, pressed down, shaken together, running over, will be put into your lap; for the measure you give will be the measure you get back. (Luke 6:38)

Kenneth H. Quigley
Senior Program Director, Endowment Management
Solutions, Episcopal Church Foundation

Fulfilling My Wishes   PG 5

Although everyone knows that our earthly life will come to an end, many people are reluctant to reflect on the legacy we wish to leave behind for our loved ones and the world. Do we wish to be remembered as people who feared death so much that we never seriously considered who would care for our children or how our worldly goods would be distributed? What types of end-of-life medical care do we wish, and whom do we want to make those decisions? Do we want people to understand who and what we valued and what institutions we believed made a transformational impact?

Sadly, a huge number of people avoid taking the time to reflect properly on these crucial issues. That avoidance can cause tremendous stress and sometimes serious harm when end-of-life plans are postponed or done without proper reflection. Who wants their heirs to argue over who should get what, or what types of medical care are desired? Not taking the time to consider what our actual wishes are and not recording them with the help of professionals will often cause great difficulty and pain to family and friends after we pass away.

For your own legacy, take the time to pause and reflect on all of your end-of-life and health care wishes, then record and discuss them with your family and those you appoint to make decisions on your behalf. Seek the help of friends and family who have done this important work already, and work with professional advisors to ensure that your legacy is not one of confusion and avoidance, but instead, clarity in your wishes, confidence in your decisions, and commitment to the people and institutions that have been important in your life.

James W. N. Murphy, CFRE
Managing Program Director, Financial Resources,
Episcopal Church Foundation

How Big Should Our Endowment Be?   PG 6

A larger church called and asked if there was a rule of thumb to determine how big their endowment should be, given their pledge and plate and membership. My answer was a question: "What's the purpose of your endowment?" If it is to support the annual operating budget of the parish, then do the math. It's pretty simple. Take 4 percent times a rolling average value of the fund. Is that sufficient? If not, you need a bigger endowment.

But if your purpose is something other than the operating budget of the parish, then the sky's the limit. A well-conceived and organized endowment breathes life into a congregation. It makes new ministries possible, sparks creative outreach projects, eases the burden of long-term capital expenses, and secures the future of our churches. Plus, from the donor's perspective, a well-ordered endowment provides a trustworthy means of making a legacy gift.

Kenneth H. Quigley
Senior Program Director, Endowment Management
Solutions, Episcopal Church Foundation

Raising to the Level of Family   PG 7

I have been privileged to hear many personal stories about the deep commitment people feel toward their parish. I remember a young woman recounting when she became a single parent and how her parish rallied around her, providing ongoing emotional support, as well as sometimes buying diapers and assisting with babysitting her daughter. To this woman, her parish literally became her support network and extended family.

In every workshop I do on legacy giving from one's estate, there is one I phrase I say consistently: "When someone makes a planned gift of any kind to their parish, that person raises their congregation to the level of family in their estate plans." Such a gift demonstrates that someone believes so strongly in the mission and ministry of their parish, that they would elevate it to the same status as one of their children or grandchildren for the eventual distribution of their worldly goods. Such a gift is not a simple token, but demonstrates tremendous passion and conviction for the future ministry of the parish.

When someone makes this choice—whether a bequest, remaining IRA balance, insurance policy, or residuum of a charitable remainder trust or gift annuity—that person offers a testimony: "I want to support my parish's future ministry and to continue to participate in the mission which became so vital during my lifetime."

Has your parish home brought you closer to God and to the people God has brought into your life? Do you want others to have an opportunity to have that same experience? Though individuals must reflect on family commitments and what fits them best, a planned gift allows anyone to become literally a part of that future ministry.

James W. N. Murphy, CFRE
Managing Program Director, Financial Resources,
Episcopal Church Foundation

This Is Your Life   PG 8

Recently, I thought about my deceased grandmother, of whom I have numerous found memories. We affectionately called her "Granny." The thing I remember most is watching one of her favorite television programs with her—"This Is Your Life." Many of you probably remember that program. It was fascinating because it centered on the special guest's life and those persons to whom they were close. Behind a curtain, someone from the person's past would share interesting stories about the special guest, and later that person would come from behind the curtain.

For several minutes, I thought about how great my grandmother was: how she helped people, how she served in her church, how generous she was, and how cheerful. Then, I began to think about how I would be remembered. Would people say that I was stingy, tight, and selfish? Would they say I only attended church occasionally, and I never served in a ministry? Maybe they would say that I was a faithful and generous servant. What will be my legacy? That's a frightening and overwhelming question.

Well, it's not too late. There is time to write the final chapters of your life. Placing your church in your will is a powerful way of leaving a legacy, while providing resources that will touch and impact lives for generations to come.

The Rev. Melvin Amerson
Methodist Foundation, Austin, Texas

The Ultimate Visionary   PG 9

Being an endowment planter (or an endowment donor) is being the ultimate visionary. The funds invested will grow and support ministries that you cannot imagine today. What ripples of good works will your endowment start? What mustard seeds will it plant? Long after all of us have passed on to our reward, what wonderful things will the endowment you funded be doing twenty years, fifty years, a hundred years from now? Endowments are the ultimate act of faith in the future of your church and its mission in the world.

From Wheaton College hymn (in the context of a church community):

A hundred years pass like a dream,
Yet early founders still are we,
Whose works are greater than they seem,
Because of what we yet shall be
In the bright noon of other days,
Mid other souls and other ways.[4]

Kenneth H. Quigley
Senior Program Director, Endowment Management
Solutions, Episcopal Church Foundation

What Gift Is Right for Me?   PG 10

From time to time, when I am asked the question, "What type of planned gift is the best?" I say one of my least favorite but most common phrases: "Well, it depends." No person or situation is exactly the same and the choice of any planned gift out of one's estate requires much reflection. Even though everyone has the ability to make a planned gift, many have never even considered it. However, if you believe that your parish has been transformational in your life and makes a difference in the lives of others, a planned gift from your estate or other assets may be the right decision for you.

The right choice for you requires reflection on your needs and context, as well as feedback from family and guidance from professional advisors. Many people need to retain their assets during their lives, but can make a significant gift by leaving a portion of their estate at death. Others may have life insurance to leave assets for their family or to charities. Still others may need additional income in retirement and may make a gift now and receive ongoing income through a charitable remainder trust or gift annuity.

---

4. Used with permission: Wheaton College Office of Legal Affairs & Risk Management.

Choosing which charity to support is usually a harder choice. Six years ago I met a woman who had quickly made a planned gift to her alma mater, but never realized she could have done the same gift for her parish. She was fully committed to her parish, working for years as its unpaid receptionist and she spent decades volunteering in its soup kitchen, though she had not visited her alma mater in over thirty years. Fortunately, she could still change her estate plans.

What gift is right for you? You will be the best judge, and your desire to pass on the blessings you have received to future generations is the most important first step.

James W. N. Murphy, CFRE
Managing Program Director, Financial Resources,
Episcopal Church Foundation

Bibliography

Berryman, Jerome M. *The Complete Guide to Godly Play*. Vol. 3. New York: Church Publishing, 2017.

The Book of Common Prayer. New York: The Church Hymnal Corporation, 1979.

Christopher, J. Clif. *Not Your Parents' Offering Plate: A New Vision for Financial Stewardship*. Nashville: Abingdon Press, 2008.

Doyle, C. Andrew. *Church: A Generous Community Amplified for the Future*. Alexandria, VA: VTS Press, 2015.

"The Expansion of Christianity: An Interview with Andrew Walls," *Christian Century*, 117, no. 22 (August 2–9, 2000): 792–95.

Gould, Meredith. "The Social Media Gospel." In *Sharing God's News in New Ways*, 2nd ed. Collegeville, MN: Liturgical Press, 2015.

LaFond, Charles. *Fearless Church Fundraising: The Practical and Spiritual Approach to Stewardship*. New York: Morehouse Publishing, 2012.

The New Oxford Annotated Bible—New Revised Standard Version. New York: Oxford University Press, 1991.

Plutarch, "Agis." In *The Lives of the Noble Grecians and Romans*. Vol. 14, *Great Books of the Western World*. Edited by Robert Maynard Hutchins. Chicago: Encyclopedia Britannica, 1952.

Indexes

Stewardship

Planned Giving

Scripture Index

Church Year Meditations—Cross Referenced

Year A and ABC

Year B

Contributing Authors

The Rev. Stacy Alan
Chaplain, Brent House, the
   Episcopal Center at the
   University of Chicago

SO	12	PG 96
SO	13	PG 96
SO	14	PG 97
SO	15	PG 98

The Rev. Melvin Amerson
The Methodist Foundation,
   Austin, TX

S	7	PG 46
S	11	PG 49
S	17	PG 53
S	27	PG 61
PG	8	PG 156

Pastor Hilarion Arenas
Tarija, Bolivia, with Five Talents
   USA

SO	39	PG 115

Mr. Brian Joseph Backe
Senior Director for U.S.
   Programs and Resource for
   Catholic Relief Services

G	13	PG 80

The Rev. Jane R. Bearden, STM,
   Hon.rt.
The Presbytery of Baltimore,
   MD

G	5	PG 74
SO	61	PG 134

The Rev. Dr. William L.
   Bearden, Hon.rt.
The Presbytery of Baltimore,
   MD

G	12	PG 80

Ms. Amanda Beyer
Senior Program Officer,
   Episcopal Migration
   Ministries

SO	29	PG 106

Dr. Mary Blair
Chair, Stewardship Team,
   Cathedral of the Incarnation,
   Baltimore, MD

G	2	PG 72
G	17	PG 83

The Rt. Rev. Joe Goodwin
  Burnett
Tenth Bishop of Nebraska,
  2003–2011
G   10   PG 78
G   22   PG 87

Mr. Jerry Campbell
Capital Campaign Consultant,
  Episcopal Church Foundation
G   4   PG 73
G   11   PG 79

The Very Rev. Stephen Carlsen
Dean and Rector, Christ Church
  Cathedral, Indianapolis, IN
S   15   PG 52
G   8   PG 77

The Rev. Suzanne M. Culhane
Canon for Stewardship, Diocese
  of Long Island
S   9   PG 47
S   18   PG 53

The Rev. Mary Davisson
Executive Director/Port
  Chaplain, Baltimore
  International Seafarers'
  Center
G   20   PG 86
G   21   PG 86

Ms. W. Lee Dickson
Executive Director, Godly Play
  Foundation, Inc.
SO   45   PG 119
SO   47   PG 121

The Rt. Rev. C. Andrew Doyle
Ninth Bishop of Texas
S   30   PG 64
S   32   PG 65

Mr. Rick Felton
The Episcopal Network for
  Stewardship
S   12   PG 49

The Rev. Canon Scott Gunn
Executive Director, Forward
  Movement, Cincinnati, OH
S   33   PG 66
G   18   PG 84

The Rev. Canon Jan Hamill
Director, Episcopal Service
  Corps, Maryland
SO   35   PG 111
SO   36   PG 112

The Rev. Dr. Thomas John
  Hastings
Executive Director, Overseas
  Ministries Study Center, New
  Haven, CT
SO   63   PG 136
SO   64   PG 137

Ms. Constance Hegarty
Retired Organist and Choir
  Director, Windsor Locks, CT
SO   2   PG 90
SO   78   PG 148

The Rt. Rev. Robert W. Ihloff
Bishop of Maryland, Retired
S   16   PG 52

The Rev. C. K. Robertson, PhD
Canon to the Presiding Bishop
  for Ministry Beyond the
  Episcopal Church

S	14	PG 51
S	21	PG 56
G	1	PG 71

The Rev. Margarita Santana
Canon for Latino Ministry,
  Episcopal Diocese of
  Maryland

| SO | 56 | PG 127 |
| SO | 57 | PG 129 |

The Rev. Regan M. Schutz
Director of Communications
  and Development, Godly Play
  Foundation, Sewanee, TN

| SO | 46 | PG 120 |
| SO | 48 | PG 121 |

Mr. Greg Sharkey
Senior Philanthropy Advisor,
  The Nature Conservancy

| SO | 27 | PG 105 |

The Rev. Dr. J. Barrie Shepherd
Minister Emeritus of historic
  First Presbyterian Church,
  New York, NY

S	1	PG 41
S	28	PG 62
S	34	PG 66

The Rev. Dr. Laura
  Sheridan-Campbell
Vicar, Holy Cross Church,
  Carlsbad, CA

| G | 6 | PG 75 |
| G | 19 | PG 85 |

Ms. Julie Simonton
Officer for Congregational
  Development and
  Stewardship, The Episcopal
  Diocese of Virginia

S	4	PG 43
S	19	PG 54
S	22	PG 57

The Rt. Rev. Eugene Taylor
  Sutton
Bishop, Episcopal Diocese of
  Maryland

| G | 9 | PG 77 |
| SO | 10 | PG 95 |

Ms. Betty Symington
Executive Director, ERICA—
  Episcopal Refuge and
  Immigrant Center Alliance,
  Baltimore, MD

SO	30	PG 107
SO	31	PG 108
SO	32	PG 108
SO	33	PG 109

The Rev. Daniel Webster
Canon for Evangelism and
    Media, Episcopal Diocese of
    Maryland
SO   38   PG 114
SO   70   PG 141

The Rev. Fred Weimert
Vice President of the Board,
    Central Maryland
    Ecumenical Council
S   8   PG 46
S   26   PG 60
S   31   PG 64

The Rt. Rev. Carl Walter Wright
VII Bishop Suffragan for the
    Armed Forces and Federal
    Ministries
SO   73   PG 143